Praise for *The New Killer Apps*

"*The New Killer Apps* is an important book for the boards and managements of every company dealing with the avalanche of technological change. I am giving the book to each director I work with."

—**Jack Greenberg**, chairman, Western Union, and former chairman and CEO, McDonald's

"This book's eight innovation rules represent the difference between big companies leveraging their assets or getting their assets whooped."

—**Guy Kawasaki**, former chief evangelist of Apple and author of *APE: Author, Publisher, Entrepreneur*

"Having observed, firsthand, the missed 'killer app' opportunity of digital imaging at Kodak and, in contrast, the multibillion-dollar success of General Motor's OnStar, I endorse with great confidence the concepts found in this book."

—**Vince Barabba**, former head of market research, Kodak; retired head of strategy development at General Motors; and former director of the United States Census Bureau (twice)

"Great work! The more I read, the more I couldn't put it down. This book is essential for any leader attempting to chart the course for a large organization."

—**Philip Fasano**, executive vice president and chief information officer, Kaiser Permanente

"Delightfully fresh, insightful and downright useful, this is the best business book I've read in very many years. It absolutely nails how to and how not to innovate."

—**Sam Hill**, author of *Radical Marketing*, former partner and chief marketing officer, Booz Allen

D0191843

"Mui and Carroll have written another 'must read.' They provide practical advice about how to be *big* and *agile* and win! They outline specific steps to overcome barriers to innovation and turn size into an advantage, and they offer compelling examples of exactly how to get it done."

—**Linda A. Hill**, Wallace Brett Donham Professor of Business Administration and Faculty Chair, Leadership Initiative, Harvard Business School

"Shift happens: If you want to make a positive, long-lasting difference in a big, long-established company, this is the book for you. Mui and Carroll offer brilliant insights and practical advice on the urgent work of making real change."

—**William C. Taylor**, cofounder, Fast Company and author, *Practically Radical*

"This book shows, step by step and with many examples, what needs to be done—and what needs NOT to be done—to foster successful, breakthrough innovation. Well-written and easy to read, it will be of interest to businesses of all sizes."

—**Dan Bricklin**, chief technology officer, Alpha Software, and cocreator of VisiCalc, the pioneering spreadsheet

"For anyone responsible for innovation at a large company, this book clears any doubt on how to use scale to win."

—**Paul Chibe**, US chief marketing officer, Anheuser-Busch Inbev

"Mui and Carroll breathe new life into what I thought was a dead horse—making large corporations innovative. Rather than chasing Silicon Valley VCs for co-investments in innovative start-ups that they'll just squander, the world's largest corporations should follow the eight-rule process in this book to nurture their own killer apps!"

—**Gordon Bell**, legendary computer engineer, prolific angel investor, and author, *High Tech Ventures*

"This book's well-researched and clearly explained rules provide a simple approach for big incumbent companies to turn transformative technologies into growth opportunities. Incumbents can indeed beat start-ups, and this important book explains how."

—**Larry Burns**, former corporate vice president, research and development, General Motors, and coauthor, *Reinventing the Automobile*

"Challenging conventional wisdom, the authors strike an optimistic note, provide great insight, and show a path for large organizations to anticipate the future and, by using the power of their considerable resources, successfully exploit it."

—**Phiroz Darukhanavala (Daru)**, vice president and chief technology officer, BP

"Chunka and Paul translate a blizzard of technological upheavals into words to live by for businesses. This book is about thinking big, staying big, and getting bigger in new ways."

—Andy Lippman, cofounder and associate director, MIT Media Lab

"Leaders who have the courage and conviction to Think Big, Start Small, and Learn Fast will be the ones who succeed in the business reinvention demanded by this era."

—**Amy J. Radin**, chief marketing officer, AXA Equitable

"Ask yourself who should be more fearless, a start-up or a big, established company? It is the latter—for they are far more able to withstand mistakes, and mistakes are where we learn the most! Lots of great lessons in this book!"

—**Greg Rayburn**, partner, Kobi Partners, and former chairman and CEO, Hostess Brands

"*The New Killer Apps* offers a compelling blueprint for established organizations that want to foster innovation and remain competitive in our rapidly changing world of start-ups and upstarts."

—**Alan Siegel**, president and CEO, Siegelvision

"Chunka and Paul do a great job of defying the notion that a company's culture of innovation and agility are related to its size. Big companies that understand this and execute are destined to succeed."

—**Peter Q. Thompson**, CEO, Perkins Investment Management

"*The New Killer Apps* illustrates the common pitfalls encountered by organizations trying to innovate and provides a simple but effective road map—Think Big, Start Small, and Learn Fast—for developing the next killer app."

—**Mikael Thygesen**, chief marketing officer, Simon Property Group, and president, Simon Brand Ventures

"This book provides a compelling case for embracing innovation and a good road map for taking advantage of the tremendous opportunities coming our way."

—**Sanjay Gupta**, executive vice president, Marketing, Innovation and Corporate Relations, Allstate Insurance Company

"Mui and Carroll offer thought-provoking cases studies and compelling rules for how large, established companies can quickly become true innovators. Given the disruptions we face, the timing of this book is perfect."

—**Robert Schifellite**, corporate senior vice president, Investor Communication Solutions, Broadridge Financial Solutions

"Can big firms master disruptive innovation? Yes, if they Think Big, Start Small, and Learn Fast, and implement this book's eight "killer rules."

—**Stephen Denning**, author of *The Leader's Guide to Radical Management*

"This book clearly, cleverly, and concisely presents the coming challenges, pitfalls, and prescriptions for success over the next decade. Take it as your wake-up call, compass, and guide to ensure you end up among the winners, rather than the many losers."

—**Toby Redshaw**, former global chief information officer, Aviva and American Express

"Mui and Carroll turn conventional wisdom on its head by showing how big companies can not only handle the disruptive innovation rearing its head in industry after industry; they can leverage it and thereby turn the tables on start-ups. Embrace their principles, apply their tools, and reap the rewards."

—**B. Joseph Pine II**, co-author, *The Experience Economy and Infinite Possibility*

"I measure the value of a business book by how uncomfortable it makes me feel. The New Killer Apps explains how to develop a mindset and a framework for surviving and thriving in a time when technology is constantly disrupting business models. It really took me out of my comfort zone - and that's a good thing."

—**Donagh Herlihy**, senior vice president and chief information officer, Avon Products

"A stunningly useful manual for getting to the future."

—**Marvin Zonis**, Professor Emeritus, Booth School of Business, The University of Chicago

For Astro —
Captain of
Moonshots!

The New Killer Apps

How Large Companies Can
Out-Innovate Start-Ups

Best Wishes,
Chu Kah

Chunka Mui and Paul B. Carroll

[ADVANCE READER EDITION]

CORNERLOFT PRESS
The New Killer Apps: How Large Companies Can Out-Innovate Start-Ups
Chunka Mui and Paul B. Carroll

Cover Design: Shawn Welch
Interior Design: Shawn Welch

Published in the United States by Cornerloft Press
ISBN-13: 978-0-9892420-1-1

Advance Reader Edition
Printed by CreateSpace, a DBA of On-Demand Publishing, LLC

Authors' Note to this Advance Reader Edition

Dear Reader,

You hold in your hands an advance preview of our latest thoughts on how large companies can successfully innovate.

This book is the progression of decades of exploration into the critical success factors and land mines of innovation, propelled by our research, consulting and management experiences. It advances the thinking of the two books that we've written separately—*Unleashing the Killer App* and *Big Blues*— and the one that we previously wrote together—*Billion Dollar Lessons.*

But, nobody is smart as everybody. We welcome your reactions to this advance edition and look forward to continuing the conversation as we continue to explore this important topic.

Best Regards,

Chunka Mui — chunka.mui@killerappsbook.com
Paul B. Carroll — paul.carroll@killerappsbook.com

September 2013

Dedication

From Chunka:

To my mom and dad, who gave up everything so that we might have something; to my sister and brothers, who helped me take advantage of that gift; and, to Beth, Kai and Zoe, with love.

From Paul:

To Mom

Contents

About The Authors

Paul Carroll spent 17 years as an award-winning reporter and editor at the *Wall Street Journal* in the US, Europe and Latin America, getting as broad an exposure to business as that world-class newspaper could give. During his time at the Journal, Paul published *Big Blues: The Unmaking of IBM* in 1993, analyzing the rise and fall of what was once the world's most profitable company.

Chunka Mui, meanwhile, led groundbreaking research on how emerging technologies would affect business. The research culminated in the best-selling *Unleashing the Killer App: Digital Strategies for Market Dominance*, which he cowrote with Larry Downes in 1998.

Our collaboration began in 1996 at Diamond Management and Technology Consultants, where Chunka was chief innovation officer and Paul directed research and publishing. At Diamond, we assisted scores of companies on radical innovation efforts.

We refined our perspectives at the Devil's Advocate Group, which we cofounded in 2008, and where we continue our research, writing and consulting. In particular, we (assisted by 20 researchers provided by our friends at Diamond) spent nearly two years examining the 2,500 major business failures that led to our 2008 book, *Billion Dollar Lessons*. We continue to help large public and private-sector organizations design and stress-test their innovation strategies.

Acknowledgments

L ong ago, we settled on a motto based on a line we appropriated from a friend's book. (After all, what are friends for?) The line: Nobody is as smart as everybody.

While that is surely true in general terms, we have benefited from that motto more than most could because we have so many friends and colleagues who are not only remarkably smart but are willing to invest hours and even days of their time in making us smarter.

To all of you: Thank you so very much. You have made this book far better than it would have been otherwise while providing the friendship and support to keep us going through draft after draft over the past three years.

We'd especially like to thank those who have helped us test our ideas in the real world and forge them into concepts that provide "killer"impact. Among them: Tom Wilson, Joan Walker, Sam Hill, Tom Warden, Jeff McRae, Bob Schifellite, Michelle Jackson, Chuck Callan, Lyell Dampeer, Doug DeSchutter, Joe Vicari, Dev Parekh, Cathy Conlon, Patricia Rosch, Rob Krugman, John Oliveri, Bernie Hengesbaugh, Ken Sharigian, and Jim Madara.

For sheer patience, the award has to go those who gave us a sort of blank check, offering to keep reading drafts as we kept honing our thinking. They may not have realized just how much we would follow our Think Big, Start Small, Learn Fast approach—with all the testing that entailed and with the willingness to jettison what wasn't working, even to the point of throwing out a manuscript that we hoped was finished and rewriting it at half the length, with numerous new examples. But these folks were as good as their word, offering valuable feedback at frequent intervals. Thank you to: Kirsten Sandberg, Toby Redshaw, Nick Pudar, Vince Barabba, Dan Roesch, Alan Kay, Gordon Bell, and Larry Smarr.

They may have learned their lesson and may never give us such a blank check again, but they sure did this time.

Thanks, too, to all those who read the full draft and offered detailed comments. These folks remind us of a story that Paul tells from his days as a reporter. Someone he interviewed once began with an unusual preamble. He said, "I don't need my name in this story, so we aren't talking off the record or even on background. We're just talking because we both want Paul Carroll to look smarter in tomorrow's Wall Street Journal." The folks who read the full draft do get a brief reference here but spent far more time and effort on making us smarter than we could ever really acknowledge. Among them: Astro Teller, Adam Gutstein, John Sviokla, Vaughn Kauffman, Valter Johansson, Tim Swords, Tom Waite, Steve Gaubatz, Rob Moon, Phil Sachs, Mark Zawacki, Malcus Watlington, Lynne Whitman, Lynda Cotter, Lee Wachter, Larry Bleiweiss, Lai Nin Wan, Jack Greenberg, Greg Gleason, Guy Kawasaki, Frank Orzell, John Thomson, Jeffrey Schuchert, Lynn Whitehorn, Brian Finucane, Laura Adams, Steve Van Erman, Mike Razzoog, Alan Matsumura, Brad Power, Bob Barrett, Belden Menkus, Anne Miller, Alex Nedzel, Alan Siegel, Andy Lippman, Caroline Calkins, Dan Bricklin, Phiroz Darukhanavala (Daru), Don Tapscott, Donagh Herlihy, Greg Brandeau, Greg Rayburn, Sanjay Gupta, Linda Hill, John Hinshaw, Mark Jamison, Joe Pine, Larry Kramer, Marvin Zonis, Mel Bergstein, Mikael Thygesen, Nicholas Negroponte, Paul Chibe, Paul Saffo, Phil Fasano, Amy Radin, Peter Thompson,Bill Taylor, Les Tuerk, Jennifer Hayes Salin, Nancy Ahyee, R. Paul Herman, Jim McGee, and Courtney Young.

In addition, thanks to those who provided such good guidance as they turned a raw manuscript into the finished product you are now reading: Shawn Welch, Gretchen Dykstra, and Guy Kawasaki. We felt that, in the spirit of innovation, we needed to self-publish even though all our previous books were done with major imprints, and Shawn, Gretchen, and Guy guided us expertly on our way.

Finally, thanks to our families for letting us take all the time we needed to get this book right, ignored (mostly) the crankiness that sometimes came with the work, and provided more help and emotional support than we likely even realize. We love you guys.

Foreword

When I joined the American Medical Association as CEO in 2011, I became part of an organization with an extraordinary history and a wonderful mission ("To promote the art and science of medicine, and the betterment of public health"). Founded in 1847, the AMA brought science and professional standards to a field that was still in its snake-oil phase in the United States. In the early 1900s, the AMA spurred a review of medical schools that led to the closing of scores of diploma mills that would graduate almost anyone willing to pay. An era of thorough training for prospective physicians began. In the mid- to late twentieth century, the AMA played a major role in highlighting the links between tobacco and cancer and in shaping policy on other issues of crucial importance to the nation's health.

But, like many large and successful organizations, the AMA also built, over time, an unwieldy organizational portfolio that tried to do everything. It became difficult to capture the AMA in a focused narrative. In other words, we found ourselves in the position of many of the companies whose failure stories are chronicled in this book. We had become big and diffuse.

Meanwhile, medicine had grown enormously complex and was changing rapidly. There are now some 4,000 medical and surgical procedures and 6,000 drugs to treat 13,600 conditions that may ail our patients. Information technology is accelerating progress through the aggregation of data in electronic health records and through personalized medicine. The spread of minute sensors and powerful new medical devices (otherwise known as smartphones) are together making it possible to monitor patient conditions around the clock and providing instant connections with doctors. In the last decade, the number of genes found to be related to disease has jumped from a few to some 5,000, while the cost of genome sequencing has plummeted. At the same time, the Affordable Care Act and other laws and regulations are introducing major changes in how care is paid for and organized.

It became clear that incremental changes in how the AMA pursued its mission would be insufficient to meet the demands of this dynamic environment, and the Board of Trustees charged me with bringing impact through focus. The portfolio of approved policies formed by the 185 medical societies that constitute the AMA House of Delegates provides a rich resource from which to build focused strategies.

We're now working hard to become big and agile

To ensure that we act with agility and keep up with the pace of change in medicine, we've embraced many of the lessons on stress-testing strategies that came out of the Devil's Advocate techniques that Chunka Mui and Paul Carroll developed in their much-admired 2008 book, *Billion Dollar Lessons: What You Can Learn from the Biggest Business Failures of the Last 25 Years*. We've also begun applying the Think Big, Start Small, and Learn Fast approach to innovation that they lay out in this book. Their analysis has been enormously helpful.

As this book recommends, we took out a clean sheet of paper and imagined what the AMA would look like if it were ideally positioned to accomplish its mission. We streamlined a list of 115 strategic initiatives down to three truly strategic pillars, which we announced in 2012. We're leading the effort to bring medical education radically up to date, after almost a century of incremental change that has left medical schools out of sync with how medicine is practiced. We're working to improve health outcomes across the nation, focusing first on preventing Type

II diabetes and reducing hypertension. And we're helping physicians increase their job satisfaction and make their practices more sustainable, to ensure a continuing supply of doctors who represent the best and brightest of their generation.

Succeeding in any one of these three initiatives would represent a great step forward for our mission, but we intend to succeed in all three. So, we've been conducting other exercises laid out in these pages. For instance, Chunka and Paul helped us imagine ourselves five years into the future and developed "future histories" that crystallized our thinking about the long-term aspirations of the organization and about the challenges facing us. By producing a chronicle of what could be our major successes or our most dreaded failures, we gained clarity about the levers we need to pull to succeed and the pitfalls we need to avoid. We saw ways that the three initiatives could reinforce one another, rather than be largely independent. The exercise also helped everyone in the organization—even those not directly involved in the three initiatives—understand how they fit and could play important roles.

We've also begun developing a portfolio of potential killer apps for medicine. "Killer" and "medicine" aren't words that you often see in the same sentence, but we expect to find ways to make radical improvements for medical students, for physicians, and, most importantly, for patients.

Innovation is hard. It may actually be harder in successful organizations because they have developed such a clear way of doing things that it may be difficult to adapt to a changing environment. Certainly, at the AMA, we have a strong culture that has served us well for more than a century and a half, but we must adapt if we are to keep pursuing our mission in a world where so much is changing.

The book you hold in your hands offers a very smart approach to innovating in confusing times, even if you're a large organization with a long history of success doing things a certain way—actually, especially if you're a large organization with a long history of success.

James L. Madara, M.D.

CEO, American Medical Association

The New Killer Apps

~ *Introduction*
Big and Agile Beats Anyone— A Road Map for Corporate Innovation

This book aims to reverse a bit of conventional wisdom that's taken root in recent decades: that start-ups are destined to out-innovate big, established businesses. The conventional wisdom just isn't true. Or, at least, it need not be. Yes, small and agile beats big and slow, but big and agile beats anyone—and that combination is now possible.

We say that based on the lessons we've learned during three decades of writing, researching, and consulting on innovation with giant, established institutions. Since the start of the Internet boom some two decades ago, so many companies have looked to information technology to innovate that there's now a track record showing what works and what doesn't. Having studied hundreds of those efforts—and lived through many of them—we're ready to apply those hard-earned lessons to the new wave of technological capabilities now before us.

The possibilities are startling. And tapping into them isn't optional. Being big and agile isn't just feasible; it's essential.

A perfect storm of six technological innovations—combining mobile devices, social media, cameras, sensors, the cloud, and what we call emergent knowledge—means that more than $36 trillion of stock-market value is up for what some venture capitalists are calling "reimagination" in the near future. That $36 trillion is the total market valuation of public companies in the ten industries that will be most vulnerable to change over the next few years: financials, consumer staples, information technology, energy, consumer goods, health care, industrials, materials, telecom, and utilities.[1] Incumbent companies will either do the reimagining and lay claim to the markets of the future or they'll be reimagined out of existence.

No history of success will protect you if you find yourself on the wrong side of innovation, and problems can appear quickly. Borders, Circuit City, Blockbuster, and many others went from thriving business to out of business in almost no time. Think of how recently Nokia and BlackBerry were on top of the world and how they're now irrelevant. The near future will be even more brutal and more lethal, with faster cycle times.

That may sound like the kind of thing people always say: Every catastrophe is the worst ever, every breakthrough the biggest ever. In fact, in a world of exponential change like technology, each new wave of innovation, which comes along every ten years or so, *is* the most disruptive ever. That's because of a phenomenon sometimes called "the second half of the chessboard."

The name refers to a story about a king who told an adviser he could name his own reward for some stunning achievement. The adviser asked for what sounded like a modest prize—just one grain of rice on the first square of a chessboard, followed by twice that many on the next square, twice as many on the next, and so on until there was rice on all sixty-four squares. By the time half the board was covered, however, the total grains of rice would have exceeded four billion, and

---

1   Nicholas Carlson, "Mary Meeker's Latest Stunning Presentation about the State of the Web," *Business Insider,* May 30, 2012, http://www.businessinsider.com/mary-meekers-latest-incredibly-insightful-presentation-about-the-state-of-the-web-2012-5#-86.

the board would have been on its way to holding grain equal in weight to a million fully loaded aircraft carriers. (According to some versions of the story, the adviser was also on his way to losing his head, because he was clearly too smart for his own good.) Each new square contained one more grain of rice than the total amount on all preceding squares. In other words, each new placement of rice more than doubled what was already on the board. That doubling might not have meant much in the early stages, but it became overwhelming once the king got to the second half of the chessboard.

The same is true of Moore's Law, which states that the number of transistors on a chip will double approximately every two years. Each new generation builds on what came before and represents as much innovation as occurred in all prior generations combined. And we're now on the second half of the chessboard. The changes documented by Moore's Law didn't matter much when the number of transistors was doubling from two to four, or from sixty-four to 128, but there are now hundreds of millions of transistors on single chips, and the power is spreading in all directions—including into the six technologies that we expect to lead the new wave of innovation.

So the pace of innovation is about to surge. Again. And more powerfully than ever before.

Even Walmart, which has historically put so much pressure on so many businesses, faces a heightened attack from online retailers because of the six technologies, principally mobile devices and cameras. A study found that Amazon's prices are, on average, 19 percent lower than Walmart's.[2] While someone in a Walmart wouldn't have known that a few years ago, a practice known as "showrooming" has taken hold among consumers: They look at items in a physical store but check online prices on a mobile phone before they buy and, if the difference is great enough, order from the electronic retailer. With customers who

---

2   "Walmart vs. Amazon," *Minyanville,* June 20, 2011, http://www.minyanville. com/special-features/articles/infographic-walmart-infographic-amazon-info-graphic-amazon/6/20/2011/id/35159?camp=syndication&medium=portals&-from=yahoo.

are willing to share their location via the GPS in their smartphones, Amazon could even know that someone was checking a price while standing in a Walmart and lower the price to accentuate the difference. The Amazon price advantage will diminish as it begins collecting sales taxes in more states, but Amazon will retain a huge advantage because of the extreme efficiency of its centralized model. Best Buy has already wilted under pressure from e-tailers such as Amazon, which generates $900,000 of revenue per employee per year versus Best Buy's $200,000.[3]

America's higher-education system, long the envy of the world, may be forced kicking and screaming into radical change as technology makes college courses widely available online at a fraction of today's costs. One critic, writing in the policy magazine *The American Interest,* predicts that within fifty years, half of the 4,500 colleges and universities in the United States will be out of business and tens of thousands of professors will be out of work. Meanwhile, the critic says, the gold standard will be so highly valued that Harvard will enroll ten million students a year.[4]

Although established organizations sometimes seem resigned to the possibility that new technologies and start-ups will overrun them, the problems that have stifled innovation in large companies are now known and can be avoided. These problems are not inherent to bigness. Incumbents should be optimistic that they'll beat the start-ups this time around.

3   Jeff Jordan, "The Case for E-Commerce Acceleration (a.k.a. Bye-Bye, BBY?)," *All Things D,* June 28, 2012, http://allthingsd.com/20120628/the-case-for-e-commerce-acceleration-a-k-a-bye-bye-bby/?mod=tweet.

4   Nathan Harden, "The End of the University as We Know It," *American Interest,* January/February 2013, http://the-american-interest.com/article.cfm?piece=1352.

For one thing, start-ups aren't all they're cracked up to be. Yes, Silicon Valley has the cachet, but Harvard Business School research shows that the failure rate for start-ups runs as high as 95 percent.[5] Start-ups, as a group, succeed largely because there are so many of them, not because of any special insight.

Vinod Khosla, a billionaire venture capitalist and cofounder of Sun Microsystems, tweeted a revealing line from an executive at one of his companies in 2012: "Entrepreneurs really are lousy at predicting the future....VCs are just as bad."

What's more, the National Bureau of Economic Research (NBER) found that start-ups shift rewards to financiers while saddling entrepreneurs with most of the risk.[6] Venture capitalists sometimes do very well, but start-ups rarely pay off for the entrepreneurs who slave away at them. Entrepreneurs invest their time, reputations, and accumulated expertise for modest salaries and long hours in the hope of gaining huge rewards at "exit," when the start-up goes public or is acquired. NBER researchers found, however, that 68 percent of companies that reached an exit (after a median time of forty-nine months from first venture funding) resulted in no meaningful wealth going into the pockets of the entrepreneurs. If financiers continue to stack the odds in their favor, interest in start-ups will decline. Prospective entrepreneurs will find other intriguing alternatives to starting a business, such as helping market leaders to reimagine themselves.

The second reason that we focus our innovation work on incumbents is that they *should* win. Yes, we all know that big companies are sometimes complacent about threats, especially if those threats start small. But big companies have everything they need to continue to dominate: unmatched people, resources, supply and distribution capa-

5   Carmen Nobel, "Why Companies Fail—and How Their Founders Can Bounce Back," *Working Knowledge* (Harvard Business School), March 7, 2011, http://hbswk.hbs.edu/item/6591.html.

6   Robert E. Hall and Susan E. Woodward, "The Incentives to Start New Companies: Evidence from Venture Capital," *National Bureau of Economic Research*, April 2007, http://www.nber.org/papers/w13056.

bilities, brand power, and customer relationships. And in the context of today's immense technological opportunities, incumbents have growth platforms that would take start-ups years to build. Incumbents have products with which to leverage new capabilities such as mobile devices, networks, the cloud, cameras, and sensors. Social media can amplify their brand power and customer relationships. Incumbents already sit on mountains of market and customer data and are therefore in the best position to extract knowledge from it. Incumbents just have to get out of their own way and marshal their resources appropriately.

In this book, we've taken our experience with thousands of innovation efforts—both successes and failures—and distilled it into eight simple rules that help incumbents stay ahead of start-ups and continue to thrive even in a confusing, rapidly morphing world.

While we'll talk mainly about big businesses, because that's where our research and other work has focused, these rules can be applied to companies of any size, from Walmart all the way down to the local cigar shop. The scale of the problems and opportunities differs, obviously, but the process of innovating is quite similar. Also, while we'll focus on the role of senior management, the principles we describe apply to anyone in an organization at any level who's concerned with innovation and wants to contribute to it.

These rules apply to both defense and offense. The defense, based on two years of research on 2,500 failures that our team conducted for *Billion Dollar Lessons* (2008), identifies the major junctures where innovation efforts often falter. The offense comes out of work that went into *Unleashing the Killer App* (1998), Chunka's pioneering best seller on how information technology must drive corporate strategy. That book, written with Larry Downes, took the concept of a killer app out of Silicon Valley and introduced the rest of the business world to the idea of products so revolutionary that they cause massive creative destruction and huge shifts in revenue and market value. The book also laid out prescient concepts such as the Law of Disruption, which states that, while people change incrementally, technology improves exponentially; so, from time to time, technology will get so far ahead of people that an earthquake will have to happen to get the tectonic plates back into alignment.[7]

Unleashing the Killer App explained why transaction costs like those represented by insurance agents face withering pressure, presaging the success of agentless insurers GEICO and Progressive. The book also predicted novel marketing concepts such as giving away books to build an audience for future ones; accurately forecast a massive shift of power to consumers; and correctly argued that businesses would do away with the traditional three- to five-year forecast in favor of a more dynamic approach. In addition, the book prescribed principles such as outsourcing to the customer and building communities of value. Sure enough, today, Dell and other companies outsource much of their customer service to zealots on social media, and many incorporate customers into product development in new and profound ways. Communities of value, now expressed primarily as social media, have taken the world by storm. Fantasy sports leagues, one type of community singled out in the book, are so popular that media cover relevant stats almost as assiduously as they provide game scores. *Killer App* also warned that companies need to cannibalize their markets before someone else can and singled out newspapers and the US Postal Service as being especially vulnerable. Newspapers and the Post Office still seemed very healthy in 1998. Today? Not so much.

---

7   The Law of Disruption draws on two well-known principles in the world of information technology: Moore's Law and Metcalfe's Law. Moore's Law, named for Intel cofounder and chairman emeritus Gordon Moore, states that the number of transistors on a chip will double approximately every two years. This principle has held since Moore formulated it in the mid-1960s and seems likely to hold for the foreseeable future. Metcalfe's Law, named for 3Com cofounder and Ethernet inventor Robert Metcalfe, states that the value of a telecommunications network is proportional to the square of the number of users connected to the system. The idea is that one fax machine didn't do the world any good. The second, third, and fourth created some utility, but not a lot. By the time there were a few thousand, though, the network of fax machines became so important that every big office had to have one—and adding their machines to the network increased the value even more, so that small offices needed fax machines, and soon many individuals even installed them at home.

Killer App obviously didn't get everything right. Nobody could, given the chaos of the online environment. But now we have the benefit of hindsight: We can see the results of hundreds of projects where *Killer App* principles were applied and can draw on fifteen years of subsequent research and consulting.

That body of work, together with our research for *Billion Dollar Lessons: What You Can Learn from the Most Inexcusable Business Failures of the Last 25 Years*, has helped us identify scores of examples of companies that got things right at the critical moments, as well as scores that got things wrong. Using real-world, dirt-under-the-fingernails examples, we compare the two groups and lay out the principles that will help you join the successes.

***

When we compared the successes and the failures, we found that three major issues separated them. The successful companies thought big, started small, and learned fast. The failures did not.

By Think Big, we mean that the successes considered their full range of possible futures. They debated, at a substantive level, every possibility from going out of business to building on current capabilities but moving in brand new directions. They dared to dream big, focusing on the killer apps that could rewrite the rules of a company or industry, rather than just looking for faster/better/cheaper, incremental change. The successes typically laid out a number of possible killer apps, rather than zeroing in on one.

Thinking big led Fujifilm to face up to the daunting threat from digital photography way back in the 1980s. Fuji realized that digital would mean the death of film, photographic paper, and related chemicals—and would mean the death of Fuji itself if it didn't do something. Rather than kid itself and hope it could manage the transition to digital smoothly and keep investing in the traditional businesses—the fatal mistake at Kodak—Fuji treated those businesses as cash cows that could finance new opportunities. Fuji experimented with ways to apply its photographic expertise in new areas. Film, like skin, contains collagen, and Fuji found ways to make skin creams that are sold in Asia and Europe. Fuji also started making optical films for certain flat-screen televisions. For one sort of film, which enhances the viewing angle for LCDs, Fuji has 100 percent of the market.[8] While Kodak has filed for bankruptcy, Fujifilm had a market value of $10.7 billion as of August 2013.

The failures typically thought small. Like Kodak, they assumed that some level of continued success was guaranteed and that the future would be a slightly different version of the present. This kind of thinking is common. It's human nature to see change as incremental and to think that customers will stick with us. But incremental thinking can be very dangerous. While *Killer App* warned that threats to just one revenue stream for newspapers (classified ads) could kill the business models for metropolitan papers and recommended exploration of online alternatives, many executives couldn't imagine a significant change in ad revenue or diminished interest in print. Journalists sometimes refer to themselves as "ink-stained wretches"; how could they be ink-stained if ink went away? Because newspapers rarely faced up to their looming problems or imagined new forms for delivering news, papers have been dying a death of a thousand cuts.

Successful companies Start Small after thinking big. Our research found that, rather than jumping on the bandwagon for one potentially big idea, the successes generated multiple ideas and broke them down into small pieces for testing. They deferred important decisions until they had real data. Many companies make decisions early, based on intuition, which means that experience (also known as the past) unduly influences decisions that are all about the future. Relying on intuition protects vested interests and inhibits breakthrough innova-

---

8   "The Last Kodak Moment?" *Economist,* January 14, 2012, http://www.economist.com/node/21542796.

tion. In addition, successful companies took the time to make sure that everyone—the executive team, employees, partners, agents, and even customers—was working in unison, rather than having people pay lip service to a vision while actually working at cross purposes.

By contrast, companies that failed to innovate tended to swing from complacency to panic. They thought incrementally for too long and, being late to the game, risked everything on a single idea, only to have it not pan out. That's what killed Blockbuster, which ignored Netflix's DVDs-by-mail model for years, then bet big on its own version before fully working out the economic and operational implications. Blockbuster's business model didn't work without hundreds of millions of dollars of late fees each year, but management didn't realize that until after it promised to halt the hated charges. Starting big is also what killed Ron Johnson's attempts to turn around JC Penney. Rather than take small steps to test various possibilities, Johnson plunged into a wholesale remake of the store—even though, as the developer of the Apple stores, he had experimented with every little detail for months in a mock-up of a store before going to market. Johnson also threw out Penney's long-standing sales strategy, getting rid of discounts even though he hadn't tested his new approach and even though Penney had seen a similar strategy flop a decade earlier. (*Billion Dollar Lessons* contains other examples of retailers who tried the same shift away from discounts and whose failure should have given Johnson pause.)

The lure of starting big is pervasive. For many organizations, it's so hard to get an innovation through all the approval processes that there simply isn't the energy to bring more than one idea to market. Sometimes, a CEO decides that he has an insight, and the whole organization mobilizes behind that one idea, rather than place several smaller bets. But it's crucial to Start Small.

Companies that Learn Fast take a scientific approach to innovation. They conduct extensive prototyping before they even get to the pilot phase—let alone the big rollout—so they can gather comprehensive information about their attempts at innovation and quickly analyze what's working and what isn't. The successes also develop the institutional discipline to set aside or alter projects as soon as it's clear that they're not working.

If, instead, companies swing from thinking small to betting big, they typically have neither the time nor the inclination to learn. They fall into the "it's all about implementation" trap and end up expertly implementing a failed strategy. In the research for *Billion Dollar Lessons*, we determined that fully 46 percent of the 2,500 failures we investigated never had a chance to succeed, no matter how good the implementation, yet many companies don't take the time and apply the discipline necessary to get the strategy right before beginning the rollout.

For instance, in the early 1990s, Pepsi thought it could tap into a growing concern about purity by producing a cola that was clear. The company tested the idea a bit but rushed Crystal Pepsi to market. Pepsi launched a huge ad campaign, which debuted during the Super Bowl in January 1993. Sales surged—then stopped. It turns out that consumers associate a clear soda with something like Sprite and were confused by a cola that wasn't dark, but Pepsi never took the time to learn that basic fact. Pepsi pulled Crystal Pepsi after a year.

Yum! Brands Chairman David C. Novak, who introduced the Crystal Pepsi concept, later recalled, "A lot of times as a leader you think, 'They don't get it; they don't see my vision.' People were saying we should stop and address some issues along the way, and they were right....Once you have a great idea and you blow it, you don't get a chance to resurrect it."[9]

---

9   Kate Bonamici Flaim, "The Education of an Accidental CEO: Lessons Learned from the Trailer Park to the Corner Office (Interview with David Novak)," *Fast Company*, October 1, 2007, http://www.fastcompany.com/60555/winging-it.

***

We've applied these three principles—Think Big, Start Small, Learn Fast—to the junctures that are the most important for successful innovation. The result is a set of eight rules that will help you and your team build on your experience and creativity and ensure that you're unleashing killer apps, not killer flops. Those rules are:

1. **Context is worth 80 IQ points**. As you start to Think Big, you have to understand the information-technology environment that you'll be operating in.
2. **Embrace your doomsday scenario.** In other words, investigate all possible existential threats to your business.
3. **Start with a clean sheet of paper.** This means that you should design a perfect form of your business, as a goal to work toward.
4. **First, let's kill all the finance guys.** As you Start Small, you have to make sure you don't settle on financial projections too soon; they can't be accurate, and they hamstring innovation.
5. **Get everyone on the same page.** While the tendency is to leap into action as soon as a possible killer app is identified, it's crucial to take the time to make sure everyone is on board.
6. **Build a basket of killer options.** Now, you're finally ready to start generating ideas for killer apps, but you need to invest only small amounts in them and test lots of possibilities.

7. **A demo is worth a thousand pages of a business plan.** As you begin to Learn Fast, you must stay at the demo stage—testing and learning—far longer than you normally would.

8. **Remember the Devil's Advocate.** Make sure you have a process in place so that the tough questions keep getting asked and aren't swept away as a possibility builds momentum.

Following the eight rules will make sure that you fully consider the technologies that might destroy your business. The rules will then help you do a judo flip, turning potential danger into potential value: Let the dangers savage competitors, while you use what you've learned to find new ways to serve customers. Your organization will be able to leverage all its assets while getting out of its own way—internal obstacles are often more dangerous than external competitors. Finally, the rules will let you set up and learn from small, inexpensive experiments, then get the whole organization to rally behind the successes.

You'll wind up with killer apps that may seem like science fiction but will be so compelling that they'll be adopted with lightning speed and will change the world of business more fundamentally than most people can even imagine.

We'll look at each rule in the context of a single, continuing case study: Google and its driverless car.

Google may seem like an odd choice of an innovative, established business. After all, it still seems to many like an upstart, and it operates in the rarified world of Silicon Valley. Besides, Google was caught napping when Facebook, Twitter, and LinkedIn innovated in social media. How smart can the company be about innovation beyond the search engine that got it launched? In fact, Google has long been an incumbent. It was founded in 1998, fifteen years ago as of this writing, and has been public for nine years. The company has more than 30,000 employees and hundreds of billions of dollars of market cap that it needs to protect—and expand. It's doing just about everything a big company needs to do to keep innovating. Through new projects such as the driverless car, it's demonstrating how to find killer apps even in industries that aren't thought of as being driven by the megatrends we've identified in information technology.

Google's driverless car turns out to be a great example of a potential killer app. The car feels like it comes straight out of left field. It's not just that the technology is so far-fetched; it's that innovation in cars has generally consisted of a new ad campaign or body style, not a redefinition of how cars can be used. Some will argue that driverless cars aren't possible—and the timing is, in fact, highly uncertain. Many in the auto industry won't see Google as a serious competitor, given that the company deals in bits and bytes while cars are bumpers and belts and a whole lot of other physical objects. Yet Google's driverless car puts into play some $2 trillion in revenue each year in the United States alone, by the time you add up all the revenue for carmakers, their dealers, rental car companies, body shops, insurers, health care providers, and more.

The Google car also shows how our thinking has evolved over the past fifteen years. Toward the end of *Killer App*, the prospect of a driverless car was raised, but the assumptions about the enabling technologies were wrong. The book laid out ways that roads could be made more intelligent and could control cars better than drivers could. But that approach would have required new infrastructure throughout the country—and a daunting level of investment. Switching to intelligent roads also would have required a master plan that needed to be right the first time, rather than allowing for the gradual adoption by consumers and incremental learning and adjustment that are possible with the Google car. Chastened by experience, we're much more careful about how to introduce killer apps into the market than we were in 1998. We're also more aware that, while concepts such as the driverless car can be seen well ahead of time, they play out in ways that are hard to predict. That notion of inherent unpredictability drives much of what follows in this book.

So, we'll begin the main part of the book with a case study on Google and its driverless car, to show where the dangers and opportunities are and to explore just what a shock to the system a potential killer app can be. At the end of each of the three sections—Think Big, Start Small, Learn Fast—we'll continue the case study to show Google is implementing each of those three main ideas and to show how others need to respond.

For some time now, people writing about innovation have cited some great advice from hockey legend Wayne Gretzky: Skate to where the puck is going to be, not to where it is. We think innovation needs to be even more radical than that—and it can be, if you follow the rules outlined in this book. Innovators need to invent some new space, so they and their customers can arrive at the puck at the same time.

Necessity may be the mother of invention, but invention is also the mother of necessity.

So, let's explore how you can go about not just reimagining your future, but inventing it.

~ *Case Study*

Google Cars and $2 Trillion in Auto-Related Revenue Up for Grabs

A video shows a man climbing into a small sedan and settling in behind the wheel. The car starts off—driving itself. Without the man's hands ever touching the wheel or his feet touching the pedals, the car goes smoothly around corners and halts at stop signs. The car takes the man to buy a taco at a drive-through window, then to the dry cleaners to pick up some clothes. The kicker: Toward the end of the clip, the man explains that he's 95 percent blind and never would have been able to drive himself.

This is the Google self-driving car. It has logged more than 500,000 road miles and has a driver's license in Nevada, Florida, and California; Michigan, New York, and West Virginia are considering granting a license. The car will only get better, too, by leaps and bounds, in the same way that all electronic devices do.[10]

---

10   Google, "Self-Driving Car Test: Steve Mahan," March 28, 2012, http://www.youtube.com/watch?v=cdgQpa1pUUE/.

While cars are generally thought of as an old-school, heavy-manufacturing industry, as of three years ago the largest single cost on a BMW bill of lading was software, and the Google car provides a view into the almost indescribable potential for innovation in the automobile industry. The car also offers a great case study for other industries that are facing turmoil (in other words, almost everybody).

The self-driving car could change everything about the auto experience, from the way cars are designed, made and sold, all the way through how they are used. The car might even change forever that rite of passage that begins when a teenager climbs into the driver's seat for the first time and mom or dad has to relinquish control of the car and teach the youngster to drive (minimizing yelling whenever possible).

We're not saying the Google car will necessarily succeed. There are plenty of people who view it as a high-tech misadventure by a couple of brash young multibillionaires, Google founders Larry Page and Sergey Brin. But the car provides a useful proxy for looking at the disruption that is surely coming to cars, so let's at least consider Google's claims for the car:

- We can reduce traffic accidents by 90 percent.
- We can reduce wasted commute time by 90 percent.
- We can reduce the number of cars by 90 percent.[11]

To put those claims in context:

About 5.5 million motor vehicle accidents occurred in 2009 in the US, involving 9.5 million vehicles. These accidents killed 33,808 people and injured more than 2.2 million others, 240,000 of whom had to be hospitalized. These accidents were the leading cause of death for people ages five to 35 in the US.

---

11   Sebastian Thrun, "Google's Driverless Car," TED conference, March 31, 2011, http://www.youtube.com/watch?v=bp9KBrH8H04.

The American Automobile Association studied crash data in the ninety-nine largest urban areas in the United States and estimated the total accident-related costs—including medical costs, loss of productivity, legal costs, travel delays, pain, and lost quality of life—to be $299.5 billion. Adjusting those numbers to cover the entire country suggests annual costs of about $450 billion.

Now take 90 percent off these numbers. Google claims its car could save almost 30,000 lives each year on US highways, prevent nearly two million additional injuries, and reduce accident-related expenses by at least $400 billion a year. From the standpoint of all those who would have been injured or killed, and all those who would pay, those numbers represent glorious aspirations. But one person's savings are another person's lost revenue.

So, Google says its car will take hundreds of billions of dollars a year away from hospitals, car-repair businesses, car dealers, lawyers, and many others. While car sales might initially boom as the fleet shifted to driverless cars, they would soon fall off a cliff—and new and used car sales add up to a $600 billion-a-year business in the United States. Spending on highway construction would plummet. Gasoline sales would tumble not only because there would be fewer cars but because they would operate more efficiently—among other things, cars on highways would be able to travel in what are being called platoons, drafting off one another; they could be just inches apart because the lead car could instantaneously trigger the brakes in all the cars if it needed to slow or stop.

Auto insurers, which collect more than $200 billion in premiums each year in the United States, would initially see profits rise as accidents declined and payments to customers dropped but would eventually see something like 90 percent of premiums disappear. Health insurers would also have to give up revenue as car-related injuries plummeted. Governments would lose fines, because cars would all obey traffic laws, but police forces would need fewer officers on the road, and prisons would need less capacity as drunk drivers kept their freedom. Utilities would lose revenue because traffic lights would no longer be needed, and highways and streets wouldn't need to be lit—after all, the cars can see in the dark. Parking lots, which cover a third of the ground in some cities, would pretty much disappear, while freeing land and reducing property values. And so on.

Add up all the pieces—$450 billion in crashes, $600 billion in car sales, $200 billion in auto-insurance premiums, hundreds of billions of dollars in health insurance, and so on—and you pretty easily get to the $2 trillion that we figure is the revenue associated with cars each year in the United States. Just about all of that revenue could be taken away from the incumbents.

On the plus side, if Google is right about how much wasted commute time it can eliminate, it will save Americans four billion hours a year. They'll do something with that time, whether it's spending more time with their families, working more, or just getting to know their smartphones better. Without having to worry about distracted driving, electronics companies and app developers could outfit cars with all the distracting entertainment they wished and earn billions off the now-free time in self-driving cars.

Lots of opportunities to coordinate use of cars would appear: Cars could go from being a product to being a service that takes you someplace or that transports goods for you. Autos could also be viewed as a platform, rather than as individual vehicles. Cars make great antennas, and they have all the battery power they need for communication, so it would be easy to integrate them with each other. The companies that take advantage of these new opportunities will win, while those that maintain the status quo will see their businesses fade, if driverless cars have anything like the projected impact.

But how much of a game changer is the driverless car? Let's look.

The Google car is operated by on-board software imbued with artificial intelligence (AI) capabilities, with a human in the driver's seat, able to take control at any point. While AI had a bad reputation for decades because it failed to live up to grandiose claims about rendering humans obsolete, the field is now delivering on its early promise, and the Google car is learning effectively all the time. [12]

In other words, while the car initially knew far less than a timid sixteen-year-old who just got her permit, it's basically been in driver's ed for years and for as many miles as some people drive in a lifetime. In 2008, a state-of-the-art driverless car could go two blocks on its own on a closed course at 25 mph; by 2012, a driverless car could operate in real-world conditions at 75 mph. The car will only keep learning and getting better, too—unlike humans, many of whom work to get a license but then lapse into bad habits. With the advent of the driverless car, some scientists find it amazing that humans are even allowed to drive.

If Google cars move into widespread use, the software will keep learning from all the cars on the road, and every car will be updated with that new knowledge. That's a key point: While we humans learn almost entirely from our own experiences, every Google car can learn from the experiences of every other Google car. If we start to see hundreds, then thousands, then millions of Google cars on the road, that learning will accelerate.

---

12   Initially, AI scientists tried to develop rules that governed everything an expert would do when playing chess, using industrial equipment or whatever. It turned out that the rules couldn't cover every situation, so problems always arose. Now, scientists have moved away from the top-down approach and are going bottom up. AI systems learn a bit at a time by observing how experts act, and they keep refining that learning. With the Google car, the new approach means programmers don't write explicit instructions in code, for example, "In a roundabout, yield to cars to your left." Instead, Google uses a machine learning method that lets the software evolve based on real-life situations, sometimes watching a human drive and sometimes taking control, with a human monitoring and making corrections.

The learning won't just be about how to drive—it will be about the roads themselves. The Google car uses detailed maps to navigate, and, if Google puts massive numbers of cars on the road, those maps will improve rapidly while providing incredibly detailed, up-to-the-second information to the cloud about road conditions, traffic, and travel times. Each car will draw on that information and know to be extra careful at dangerous intersections or know, say, that there's black ice at a certain spot just ahead.

While the Google car drives itself based on data captured by cameras, radar sensors, and laser range finders that currently cost tens of thousands of dollars per car, all those devices are electronic, so their prices will keep falling rapidly even as capabilities increase. A gigabyte of memory cost $300,000 in 1981, but less than $10,000 a decade later, less than $10 a decade after that, and less than 10 cents today. From $300,000 to a dime in three decades—that's the trajectory of the electronics in the driverless car. Over time, all sorts of costs will come out of cars because they'll no longer need safety features such as airbags or bumpers and heavy frames designed to protect passengers in crashes, and so on. What's not to like?

Even skeptics seem to believe that, when it comes to the driverless car, the question is less *if* than *when*. Nissan CEO Carlos Ghosn says driverless cars will be in Nissan showrooms by 2020. A prominent engineering group estimates that 75 percent of cars will be driverless by 2040.[13]

And, *when* is less about the technology itself than a long list of legal, policy, and social challenges. There are two main ones. First, people are accustomed to driving and would, at least initially, find it hard to let go. Second, legal liability for automakers could be huge if a malfunctioning car injured or killed people.

13   Doug Newcomb, "You Won't Need a Driver's License by 2040," *Wired*, September 18, 2012, http://www.cnn.com/2012/09/18/tech/innovation/ieee-2040-cars/index.html?npt=NP1.

Personal habits will surely slow adoption, but people will come to trust the cars as evidence of effectiveness piles up. New drivers, raised with the idea that cars can drive themselves, might be more trusting than older drivers. After all, lots of people used to be scared witless about flying, but that issue has largely faded.

The liability issue is trickier—computers are completely capable of flying planes, including takeoffs and landings, yet, for liability reasons, every commercial flight has two human pilots. A study by Rand Corp. concluded that existing liability case law "does not seem to present unusual liability concerns for owners or drivers of vehicles equipped with autonomous vehicle technologies." Instead, the study predicted that the decrease in the number of accidents and the associated lower insurance costs would encourage drivers and auto insurers to adopt the technology—unlike with airplanes, where deaths are rare, there are tens of thousands of preventable deaths in cars each year.[14] A recent study found that one-third of drivers never even engaged their brakes before an accident and that 99 percent didn't engage them fully.[15] Surely, sophisticated electronics can do better.

The Rand study suggested that government might intervene and mandate self-driving cars if they prove to be half as safe as Google claims. After all, almost 370,000 people died on American roads between 2001 and 2009[16]—that is more than one and a half times as many as died in combat during the American Civil War. Although there are too many imponderables to imagine that the US government would get involved anytime soon, one can imagine scenarios where more interventionist governments, like China's, might intervene. Developing

---

14   One factor that might stem a potential flood of lawsuits is that the Google car's cameras and sensors will capture copious video and telemetry evidence about any accident. There will be no doubt about who did what to whom when.

15   Joseph B. White, "Self-Driving Cars Spark New Guidelines," *Wall Street Journal*, May 30, 2013, http://online.wsj.com/article/SB1000142412788732372820457851 5081578077890.html.

16   Tom Vanderbilt, "Let the Robot Drive: The Autonomous Car of the Future Is Here," *Wired*, January 20, 2012, http://www.wired.com/magazine/2012/01/ ff_autonomouscars/all/1.

countries actually have much greater incentives to adopt driverless cars because their rates of accidents and fatalities per 100,000 miles of driving are far greater than in the United States. Driverless cars could well take hold in a developing country, get the kinks worked out, and then take over in the United States and other developed nations.

The Google car may not soon be on the road in numbers sufficient to revolutionize the auto industry, but it offers both earth-shattering possibility and highly uncertain timing—in other words, an opportunity to either make or lose an awful lot of money on a killer app.

Even if the Google car takes a metaphorical 100 mph crash into a wall, it's an amazing experiment that will spin off loads of innovation. If driverless cars can't prevent almost all crashes, technological assists will still soon be available that can take control of a car and stop accidents in the two scenarios where various studies find it's most likely to happen: at speeds below 37 mph, in traffic, and at high speed on highways. A combination of video and sensors is being used to monitor fleets of trucks to ensure that the drivers are being careful and to capture the few seconds before and after teen drivers make risky maneuvers, so parents can use those teachable moments to make their children safer behind the wheel.[17]

Plenty of other technologies could also disrupt the car business. For instance, companies that sell navigation systems, DVD screens, and other electronics for cars will find many capabilities migrating into smartphones and tablets. Ford has already announced that it will equip some cars with a smartphone jack and skip the pricy navigation systems that have been going into many models.

That's just the changes for automakers. Every company that plays a role in the auto world will have to prepare for major change. And big changes can happen long before driverless cars become pervasive. Studies have found that a relatively modest form of accident-preven-

---

17   DriveCam home page. http://www.drivecam.com/our-markets/family/over-view.

tion technology—adaptive cruise control—needs to be in only 20 to 25 percent of cars on the road for there to be a sharp drop in accidents[18] and in the revenue of carmakers, car dealers, insurers, body shops, attorneys, and others with business that stems from collisions.

The Google car is the work of a mere twelve engineers, and the company has spent perhaps $50 million on the project,[19] yet the car gives the company a shot at a major role in a $2 trillion-a-year ecosystem. With that much revenue at stake, and innovation so inexpensive these days, every conceivable player will take a shot at upending the car business. Intel, for one, has announced a $100 million Connected Car Fund to experiment with driverless technologies.[20]

The question—the central question of this book—is how to help traditional companies soak in all the innovation that's going on, combine it with their enormous advantages, and outpace newcomers, continuing to dominate in the brave new world that they will help shape.

18   "Relieving Congestion with Adaptive Cruise Control," *The Antiplanner,* December 5, 2012, http://ti.org/antiplanner/?p=7208.

19   Andy Kessler, "Sebastian Thrun: What's Next for Silicon Valley," *Wall Street Journal,* June 15, 2012, http://online.wsj.com/article/SB10001424052702303807404577434891291657730.html.

20   Eric Savitz, "Intel Capital Launches $100 Million Connected Car Fund," *Forbes,* February 29, 2012, http://www.forbes.com/sites/ericsavitz/2012/02/29/intel-capital-launches-100-million-connected-car-fund/.

PHASE ONE: THINK BIG

~ *Rule 1:*
Context Is Worth 80 IQ Points

When the uprisings in Tunisia and Egypt in 2011 were labeled "Facebook revolutions," there was surprise. How could an idea as simple as connecting friends overthrow dictators and turn nations upside down? In fact, seemingly innocent technology changes have caused upheaval for centuries.

The Gutenberg press was just a cheaper way of printing. Yet its mass production of the Bible fostered the rise of Protestant religions and produced a host of ripple effects, including challenges to monarchies across Europe that could no longer depend on the Catholic Church to establish their legitimacy.

Television knocked down the Berlin Wall. It made great video when President Ronald Reagan stood in front of the Brandenburg Gate in 1987 and said, "Mr. Gorbachev, tear down this wall," but TV had been chipping away at the foundation of that wall for years. The government in East Germany couldn't stop citizens from getting TV signals from the West. Residents of East Berlin saw how shabby their lives were in comparison with those living just on the other side of the wall.

It should come as no surprise that social media can bring down dictators. The only real surprise is that so many people are still in denial about the power of new technologies to rewrite the rules of commerce. Even when people think they believe—having seen Blockbuster, Borders, and others fall by the wayside—they seldom see that they're next in the line of fire. If technological innovation could take down

Hosni Mubarak and his army of hundreds of thousands, what makes your business so safe? By contrast, if a few dissidents in Tunisia, then Egypt, then Libya, then Egypt again, can use new technologies to change the course of history, just imagine what you can do with them.

If you believe, as we do, the axiom by personal-computing pioneer Alan Kay[21] that "context is worth 80 IQ points," then the way to start to Think Big has to be to understand the technology context for the next five to ten years. If you don't understand the context, you'll wind up playing catch-up—the vast majority of CIOs, for instance, didn't understand even four or five years ago that they needed to start developing apps for mobile devices, and they're still scrambling. If you understand the context, you give yourself a chance to lead, maybe even dominate.

As the Google driverless car is demonstrating so dramatically to those in the auto world, you have to not only keep a handle on all the traditional forces in your industry but also come to grips with six technological megatrends: mobile devices, social media, cameras, sensors, cloud computing, and emergent knowledge.

Mobile Devices

The smartphones and tablets that are fast becoming ubiquitous represent the third wave of personal computing. The first gathered momentum in the 1980s as personal computers came into widespread use. The second wave connected all those computers together through the Internet, beginning in the mid-1990s. The third wave is now letting everyone take computing power and the Internet with them wherever they go.

---

21   While we generally avoid referring to people multiple times in this book, lest we force you to continually cross-reference names and produce something akin to a Russian novel, Kay will be a recurring figure. He is widely acknowledged as the father of the personal computer thanks to his contributions to computer design (he was the first to conceive of the personal computer), graphical user interfaces (he invented much of the approach that underpins both the Macintosh and Windows operating systems), and programming languages. He has been a friend and colleague for decades and has said an astonishing number of insightful things.

Throughout the world, more people now have mobile devices than have electricity or access to safe drinking water.[22] Ericsson predicts that by the end of the decade 50 billion devices will be connected and communicating with one another. Roughly 20 percent will be cell phones and tablets. Some 80 percent will be devices that talk to one another but not to us humans.[23]

As you think about the implications for the future, it's important to consider all the ways that mobile devices will improve even as they spread:

- **Power.** Even though humans have a hard time visualizing exponential improvement, Moore's Law guarantees that the chips at the heart of mobile devices will double in power about every two years. That means that, even if nothing else changes, your smartphone five years from now will be more powerful than your laptop is today.

- **Physical limitations.** Our limitations will still be there because of our fat, little fingers and our eyes' need for big-enough screens (especially for those of us of a certain age), but devices will overcome those limitations. Already, there are larger keyboards that can hook up to smartphones or tablets. Larger and better screens are in the works, too, including some that will unfold and be several times as large as those we currently use on our mobile devices. New technol-

---

22 Jay Yarow, "Chart of the Day: More People Have Mobile Phones than Electricity or Drinking Water," *Business Insider,* April 30, 2012, http://articles.businessinsider.com/2012-04-30/tech/31488477_1_electricity-phones-twitter.

23 Kevin J. O'Brien, "Talk to Me, One Machine Said to the Other," *New York Times,* July 29, 2012, http://www.nytimes.com/2012/07/30/technology/talk-to-me-one-machine-said-to-the-other.html?pagewanted=all.

ogies such as voice recognition like Apple's Siri and head-mounted displays like Google's Project Glass might eventually obviate the need for keyboards and screens altogether.

- **Bandwidth.** Bottlenecks will go away. Mobile network operators are rapidly building out 4G (fourth-generation) cell phone networks, which use spectrum some ten times more efficiently than the 3G networks that most smartphones use today. When we get to 5G, it will be possible to transmit an entire movie in less than a second. Meanwhile, regulators will free up huge swaths of wireless spectrum, and new technologies, like "smart radios," will let devices share spectrum much more efficiently. Essentially, we should all work on the assumption that wireless capacity is infinite. That would mean that our entire communications infrastructure would dispense with poles and wires, much as our homes are migrating away from wires in the walls.

- **Apps.** The term "smartphone" is a misnomer. Mobile devices are not smarter phones; they're platforms for apps. Mobile apps will continue to improve and proliferate. They'll also move into profound new areas. What happens when your phone is linked to sensors in your body and sends a steady stream of data for your doctor to monitor?

Research by Deloitte found that smartphones influenced $159 billion in sales in 2012 alone and predicts that figure will rise to $689 billion in 2016, primarily because of showrooming. That will be one-fifth of retail sales.[24] One of our clients, one of the largest mall operators in the world, assumes that a majority of shoppers are wandering its malls armed with mobile devices.

Showrooming can be a disadvantage—or an advantage. Tesco leased wall space in South Korean subway stations and put up displays that look like shelves in Tesco's grocery stores. As people wait, they use their smartphones to scan barcodes and put items in their virtual shopping carts. The items are delivered shortly after the commuters get home. Tesco's Homeplus line of stores went from a modest share of the South Korean grocery market to the number two share. (We have friends who desperately want someone to set up a similar system at New York's Grand Central Station so they could scan a bar code and order dinners that they could pick up at the station as they get off the train at the end of their commutes.)

The guiding principle in thinking about mobile devices: Every person and every device will be able to talk to every other person and device, instantly and at zero cost.[25] You have to figure out how you can turn this level of efficiency into an asset, rather than a liability, for your business.

---

24 Bill Siwicki, "'Showrooming' Is Adding to, Not Taking Away from, Store Sales," *Internet Retailer*, June 28, 2012, http://www.internetretailer.com/2012/06/28/showrooming-adding-not-taking-away-store-sales.

25 To get a handle on what we mean by having zero or infinite capability, a friend suggests going through an exercise he calls "backcasting the future." You pick a time frame and look at what capabilities a mobile phone, say, had at the time. Then you try to put yourself in that moment and imagine how you'd react if you had today's phone in your hand. The state-of-the-art cell phone in 2000, for instance, was notable mostly for the candy colors that Nokia used for the case. It had a teensy screen designed solely for phone numbers. It operated on a slow, 2G network with big dead zones. And, of course, there was no such thing as an app or an iTunes Store. Today's phone certainly doesn't feel infinitely powerful to you and doesn't have zero cost, but imagine if someone had given it to you in 2000. Now project that feeling of awe forward and imagine what your mobile device will be like in a decade-plus.

Social Media

Much has been written about the power of social media, but to fully grasp the implications you need to understand David P. Reed's work and what has become known as Reed's Law. Reed, one of the original architects of the Internet, proposed his law as a way to explain the math of social media, or what Reed calls "group forming networks." People tend to be allergic to math in books, so we won't lay out the whole argument here. We'll just say that Reed shows why social networks beat out other types of networks. Broadcast networks allow one source to transmit a message to hundreds of millions, which is obviously a very powerful capability and which has given us television and traditional publishing. Person-to-person networks, which include e-mail, fax machines, and the traditional phone system, turn out to be even more powerful because they allow those hundreds of millions to communicate with one another, rather than follow a single broadcast. Reed's group-forming networks are the most powerful of all because they go beyond allowing people to communicate individually to letting them form groups based on relationships or any other sort of affinity. We get to satisfy our very human need to belong to groups, such as our self-defined group of friends on Facebook, our college or corporate alumni groups on LinkedIn, and our connections on Twitter. Reed's Law explains why AOL won in the early days of the Internet, how eBay dominated auction-based commerce, and how Facebook beat MySpace.[26]

Social media would seem to be heading toward maturity. Facebook, for instance, already has a billion users. In fact, as the proliferation of social media platforms shows, the technology is likely just getting started and could head in any number of intriguing directions:

---

26   David P. Reed, "Weapon of Math Destruction: A Simple Formula Explains Why the Internet Is Wreaking Havoc on Business Models," *Context*, Spring 1999, http://web.archive.org/web/20071008165706/www.contextmag.com/setFrameRedirect.asp?src=/archives/199903/digitalstrategy.asp

- **Leveraging employees' social media connections.** While corporations mainly play defense when it comes to social media, making sure employees aren't wasting endless hours on Pinterest or inadvertently divulging trade secrets, they'll figure out how to play offense, too. Surely, some company is going to break the code and find ways to use employees' social connections to generate lots of revenue. Heavily financed start-ups such as Hearsay Social may already be on the way. Hearsay Social helps big companies provide material that representatives use to engage with customers via social media and helps sense when they might be interested in a purchase of, say, auto or life insurance. Hearsay is going beyond social marketing and assisting with social selling, promising to end cold calls forever.
- **Sharing different kinds of information.** The conversations will expand beyond talking about our vacations on Facebook or sharing interesting tidbits on Twitter. Perhaps those interested in investing will start sharing the kind of information that they previously paid financial advisers to provide. Already, medical patients are helping each other by sharing information on specialized social sites, such as PatientsLikeMe.com and Crohnology.com.
- **Using customers' physical locations.** Customers may be willing to provide their physical locations in large numbers in return for incentives at stores, restaurants, or malls. While one-off deal providers Groupon and Living Social seem to have flamed out, American Express has announced a venture with Facebook that will function as a loyalty program; stores can offer deals to targeted Amex users via their Facebook pages

and start to establish a more intimate relationship.[27] Having customers voluntarily identify themselves could let physical stores recognize customers well before they come up to the cash register and hand over a credit card—giving sales clerks a way to engage people and perhaps sell more.

- **Integrating social media site log-ins** Social sites could be knit together into what Google has described as a social layer. Rather than log in separately to Facebook, LinkedIn, Twitter, and so on, people would just sign in once and be able to interact in different ways with a whole array of different groups. Start-ups such as Zapier and IFTTT are hard at work building such a layer,[28] making it easy to share services between, say, Salesforce.com, Gmail, and Basecampe. Already, if you buy movie tickets from Ticketmaster, it tries to automatically post on Facebook that you're going to see the film.

- **Developing P2P services** Social sites could develop what might be called P2P services—as in person-to-person, going beyond the traditional B2C (business-to-consumer) and B2B (business-to-business). Already, sites such as airbnb.com and RelayRides.com are trying to organize people who want to offer services to other individual—airbnb coordinating rentals of rooms or homes and RelayRides helping with car rentals.

27   "160-Year-Old American Express Out-innovates Google and Groupon," *Tech-Crunch,* July 19, 2011, http://techcrunch.com/2011/07/19/160-year-old-ameri-can-express-out-innovates-google-and-groupon/.

28   Frederic Lardinois, "Zapier Raises $1.2M Seed Round From Bessemer Venture Partners, Draper Fisher Jurvetson and Others," *TechCrunch,* October 31, 2012, http://techcrunch.com/2012/10/31/zapier-raises-1-2m-seed-round/.

Surely, there will be many other innovations, too. There are an awful lot of clever people out there who think they can make a lot of money by pushing the envelope on social interactions. Every company should think hard about how social media models might endanger—or provide new opportunities for—its business assets and models.

The guiding principle in thinking about social media: Customers are talking with one another about you and your products; how should you join that conversation?

Cameras

There was a shock in 1991 when Los Angeles police beat Rodney King. The shock wasn't that the police beat King—it was well-known that they sometimes roughed people up. The shock was that a camera was in the vicinity and that a bystander videotaped the beating. By contrast, after the bombs went off at the end of the 2013 Boston Marathon, some wondered why it took all of two days for police to come up with video of the two terrorists.

From a business standpoint, the growing ubiquity of cameras will create loads of possibilities for understanding customers. Stores will know, for instance, more than just what customers bought. Stores will know what customers *didn't* buy, by seeing what they picked up and then put down or by seeing where they paused in an aisle without buying anything.

Domino's Pizza has even figured out how to use cameras as a marketing tool. To demonstrate that it's serious about having pizzas delivered in good shape, not smashed around in the back of a car while a young driver rushes around town, Domino's began what it called, "Show Us Your Pizza." Any customer who was not happy with his pizza could take a picture and text it to Domino's, which would give him a credit and take up the problem with the offending store. Domino's won both ways: It improved its customer service, and it boosted its image.

Walmart uses cameras to market its low prices while slyly collecting information. Customers are told to take pictures of receipts from other stores and send them to Walmart, which calculates what the shopping trip would have cost at Walmart and sends back an itemized comparison of prices. In the process, of course, Walmart has effectively enlisted an army of people who are updating it about competitors' prices.

At the same time, the use of cameras will create thorny privacy issues. Just because Big Brother can watch doesn't mean consumers are happy to let him do so. For instance, police forces could easily issue speeding tickets by tracking how fast the cell phones inside cars were moving, but no one would tolerate that.[29]

Cameras will also put power in the hands of customers. They'll be able to document that disgusting restroom or that surly clerk, and the video will grab viewers far more than a written complaint would. If a picture is worth a thousand words, what is a video worth?

The guiding principle in thinking about cameras: Cameras can be anywhere and everywhere. Where should you use them, and how can they enhance your business rather than just expose your flaws?

Sensors

Sensors are already all around you: the GPS in your phone, the crash sensors in your car, the motion sensors that let you move your character by tilting your phone while playing Cube Runner. Sensors will end up everywhere because they cost almost nothing to add to products.

---

29   In 2009 and 2010, a high school in Lower Merion Township, an upscale suburb
      of Philadelphia, turned on webcams in the laptops that the school issued to
      students. The school used the webcams to take pictures of the students in
      their homes, to check their chat logs and to see what websites they visited. The
      school even disciplined one student for his behavior while he was at home.
      Parents were not amused. The school paid $610,000 to settle a series of lawsuits
      against it.

The results will include maps that provide a much better view of the world, and in real time. Already, services report on the speed of traffic and on backups by monitoring how fast the sensors in cell phones are moving. Cell phone companies can ignore the question, "Can you hear me now?" They just have phones across the country monitor the strength of a signal and send back reports. Weather services will soon be able to do the same thing, collecting information on temperature, humidity, and so on from phones across an area. Some say maps are becoming the canvas on which all other apps will function.[30]

The military is experimenting with sensors in clothing that would monitor wounds and transmit information back to headquarters, letting medics know what to expect when they get to an injured soldier and giving commanders a moment-by-moment picture of what's happening in a battle.[31] Companies will be able to put unobtrusive sensors on employees and track the interactions of a team, which can be compared against the interactions of successful teams and adjusted, if necessary.[32]

Some companies will find ways to get consumers to let them monitor products from store through consumption and disposal to see how long products sit on shelves and how they're used. Other companies will embed sensors that will announce that, say, a dishwasher is failing *before* it fails, delighting customers and likely changing how

---

30   Vindu Goel, "Maps that Live and Breathe with Data," *New York Times*, June 10, 2013, http://www.nytimes.com/2013/06/11/technology/mobile-companies-crave-maps-that-live-and-breathe.html.

31   Innovation News Daily Staff, "Intelligent Clothing Could Save US Military Lives," Yahoo! News, May 14, 2012, http://news.yahoo.com/intelligent-cloth-ing-could-save-us-military-lives-135328115.html.

32   Alex Pentland, "The Hard Science of Teamwork," *Harvard Business Review Blog Network*, March 20, 2012, http://blogs.hbr.org/cs/2012/03/the_new_science_of_building_gr.html?cm_mmc=email-_-newsletter-_-weekly_hotlist-_-hot-list032612&referral=00202&utm_source=newsletter_weekly_hotlist&utm_me-dium=email&utm_campaign=hotlist032612.

repair services are provided. The sensors that are going into homes as part of the Smart Grid will let them monitor electricity use and prices in real time, helping people cut costs while smoothing out major inefficiencies in power generation by utilities.

One of our clients, a large property and casualty insurer, is working on what it calls "connected" cars and homes—ones with sensors that generate important information and that can always be monitored remotely, with the owners' permission, by our client. It is feverishly working to understand the implications for underwriting, service, customer relationships, and competition.

The guiding principle in thinking about sensors: Almost anything that can be measured and monitored will be. What are the high-value measurements on which you can focus, and how might they transform your business?

Cloud Computing

The general idea of the cloud is that information technology resources can be centralized utilities that serve users via fast, pervasive networks, as opposed to local resources built and operated to serve particular users—you can get access to your files, data, software, and so on from any device and any location. The cloud is analogous to the electric grid, where generating resources are centralized and power is distributed as needed. Users need only worry about plugging into the grid, not the complexities of generation and distribution.

While cloud computing enables vast economies of scale and much greater simplicity for the users, letting them buy processing and storage capacity as they need it, the more strategic issue is that cloud computing allows for greater flexibility and lower start-up costs for innovative ideas. A client of ours, for example, was recently stymied when his technology department estimated that an innovation idea would require a $12 million technology investment before prototyping could begin. That estimate was prohibitively expensive. But a little digging uncovered more than adequate cloud-based resources for less than $15,000 a month, with the option to scale up as the experiment unfolded. The effort went forward without a hitch.

The implications of cloud computing may not seem profound. Does it really matter whether you run an application on your laptop or in the cloud? Look at the invention of the electronic spreadsheet in the late 1970s. It was just a more efficient way of doing something that could be done by hand—an idea that came to Dan Bricklin because he was tired of doing so many calculations while at Harvard Business School. Yet the spreadsheet contributed to—some say caused—the appearance of corporate raiders and leveraged buyouts in the 1980s. Suddenly, lots of sharp analysts could consider limitless possibilities just by changing the inputs in a few cells in a spreadsheet. The surge in creativity let people imagine ways of reconfiguring companies that hadn't previously been considered, then use their numbers to line up financing and reshape the world of business.

The guiding principle in thinking about cloud computing: Foundational elements of information technology will become much cheaper and easier to use. How can you use that new flexibility to innovate and change your business as fundamentally as the electronic spreadsheet did?

Emergent Knowledge

The more common name for this category is "big data," and the amount of data is certainly an issue. With people carrying their link to the cloud around with them, constantly generating information about location and behaviors, companies will have access to data streams that are hundreds of times larger than they do now. It will be important just to be able to absorb it.

But the real benefit isn't the size of the database. It's the knowledge that can emerge. President Barack Obama won reelection partly because his campaign was sophisticated about mining its data to identify prospective donors, volunteers, and voters. Among other things, the campaign ran 66,000 simulations of the election every night.[33] The Romney campaign also used data mining but suffered an embarrassing failure[34]—the campaign couldn't identify the right voters to target, the right approaches to use with them, the volunteers to target them, and so on. In other words, both campaigns used big data; it's just that the Obama campaign gleaned real knowledge from it.

The need for knowledge, not just data, is why we've preferred the term *emergent knowledge* for several years now. Television stations have been threatened recently, for instance, because of a bill that would require them to post online a rather small set of data: the rates that candidates pay for political advertising. By law, candidates get the lowest rate that the stations have granted any other advertiser, so posting the data would tell the world the minimum that the stations had accepted and would give other advertisers leverage as they tried to drive their rates toward that minimum. The data have actually been available for years, as required by law. It's just that the data were prohibitively hard to collect, because the rates were squirreled away in filing cabinets around the country. Posting the rates online, a seemingly trivial change, could sharply cut stations' profitability.

Meanwhile, opportunities are arising to understand how and what people actually read, as opposed to what they merely buy. An article with the clever headline "Your E-Book Is Reading You" points out that e-readers transmit information back to the manufacturer.

33　　Michael Scherer, "Inside the Secret World of the Data Crunchers Who Helped Obama Win," *Time*, November 7, 2012, http://swampland.time.com/2012/11/07/inside-the-secret-world-of-quants-and-data-crunchers-who-helped-obama-win/.

34　　Byron York, "In Boston, Stunned Romney Supporters Struggle to Explain Defeat," *Washington Examiner*, November 7, 2012, http://washingtonexaminer.com/in-boston-stunned-romney-supporters-struggle-to-explain-defeat/article/2512861#.UJrWEVHxzyU.

So, Amazon knows that more than 18,000 readers of the second book in the *Hunger Games* series underlined the same sentence: "Because sometimes things happen to people and they're not equipped to deal with them."[35] It's easy to imagine that a more intimate understanding of reading habits would change how people sell content, and even how we all write.

The ability to handle previously unthinkable amounts of data led the *New York Times* to publish a piece with the intriguing headline, "Just the Facts. Yes, All of Them."[36] It's about a company called Factual that has set itself the task of identifying every fact in the world and making the data available as a layer of information in search engines.

Gains in artificial intelligence, combined with these huge new sets of data, let IBM's Watson computer vanquish the two most successful human contestants in Jeopardy's history in early 2011. In the business world, Watson-like technology is being used in place of paralegals to scour massive numbers of documents in preparation for litigation and is being applied in some medical diagnoses, among other places. And the spread of sensors, cameras, and mobile devices, combined with declining storage costs, makes it possible to capture and analyze all sorts of new information.

There are three logical places to look for emergent knowledge:

- **Inside the organization** Data are the by-product of doing business. Look for large stores of customer, operational, or performance data that are thrown off by business processes or generated to meet financial or regulatory requirements.

---

35   Alexendra Alter, "Your E-Book Is Reading You," *Wall Street Journal*, July 19, 2012, http://online.wsj.com/article/SB10001424052702304870304577490950051438304.html.

36   Quentin Hardy, "Just the Facts. Yes, All of Them," *New York Times*, March 24, 2012, http://www.nytimes.com/2012/03/25/business/factuals-gil-elbaz-wants-to-gather-the-data-universe.html?pagewanted=1&_r=1&ref=business.

- **At the edges of the organization** Pay particular attention to the areas where products and networks touch the marketplace. Look for opportunities to augment your products to collect diagnostic data about them, and ways to enhance your customer interfaces to reveal preferences, as Amazon does by letting customers write reviews of their purchases.

- **Through alliances with others who hold emergent knowledge** This is, essentially, the great promise of social networks, where the vast storehouses of customer "like" information can be turned into emergent knowledge about customer preferences and needs. Think of this as a variant on the line by Sun Microsystems cofounder Bill Joy, who warned, "Not all the smart people in the world work for you." In other words, reach outside the borders of your business and see what you can do with the interesting information that others have.

The guiding principle in thinking about emergent knowledge: Previously unattainable knowledge is lurking in the data assets of your organization. How can you effectively uncover that knowledge and use it to create profits?

The Real Context: All of the Above

While it's crucial that every business look long and hard at the six key technologies—mobile devices, social media, cameras, sensors, cloud computing, and emergent knowledge—even that won't paint the whole picture.

For one thing, technological developments will keep coming—that whole "second half of the chessboard" concept. 3-D printing, for instance, could have a revolutionary effect. It's currently used to make plastic parts or small batches of metal parts, but some companies, including Nike, are starting to use 3-D, or additive, printing on a commercial scale.[37] To continue our car example, imagine the possibilities if even individual parts could be printed. Today car doors are made from sheet metal that have pieces stamped out—for the window, for instance—and are then molded or stamped into shape. But 3-D printing can produce doors that are perfectly shaped without generating any waste. In fact, the metal doesn't even need to be a uniform thickness; it can be thick where strength is needed and thin where it isn't. Lots of material costs would disappear, as would loads of labor. If whole subsystems could be printed—or someday, an entire car—the design could change radically because cars wouldn't have to be broken down into pieces that could be assembled.

As the technology matures, people will have 3-D printers at home, where they'll be able to print screws or other parts rather than run out to the hardware store. (This is close to the original concept behind 3-D printing. The Navy wanted to be able to "teleport" parts to nuclear submarines by transmitting a design that a printer could make while the sub stayed underwater.) Intellectual property will become even more confused because many physical objects will become digital. All you'll have to do is wave a scanner around a product, and your 3-D printer will reproduce it.[38]

Even with the six technologies that will shape the next round of innovation, it's crucial to not just look at them individually. They can have rich interactions that create far greater disruptions. For instance, the Google car is made possible by the interactions of at least four of the six technologies. Cameras and sensors generate the moment-by-moment inputs that let software guide the car. Maps in the cloud also

---

37   John Koten, "A Revolution in the Making," *Wall Street Journal*, June 10, 2013, http://online.wsj.com/article/SB1000142412788732406330457852281268472238 2.html?mod=WSJ_hpp_LEFTTopStories.

38   We feel prescient about 3-D printing, having first written about its prospects for the Technology column in the *Wall Street Journal* on November 15, 1989.

provide information. Emergent knowledge helps the car get better at driving, both by learning from human drivers and by drawing on publicly available information about where and when accidents occur. The car can also function as a powerful, mobile communications device.

Here's one more example, just to show that nothing is sacred: Cameras and emergent knowledge may transform professional basketball. Some teams have installed tiny cameras in the rafters and have adapted missile-tracking technology from Israel to follow movement by players and the ball on the court. The teams are now able to do detailed analysis and are learning about the dynamics that lead to good shots or strong defense. The teams that get the analysis right could make the kind of step-function increase in performance that Oakland A's made a decade-plus ago and that was described in the book and movie *Moneyball*.

So, companies must not only think through each of the six technological megatrends we've listed here, but also imagine a range of potential interactions.

The first step in evaluating the range of possible interactions is to keep abreast of emerging technologies that might affect core products and key markets. This is relatively straightforward. Even mainstream publications like the *Wall Street Journal* and *New York Times* may cover technological breakthroughs in enough detail to generate effective technology road maps.

Our research found that problems arise when companies pay too little attention to what might change over time. Kodak did a study in 1981 that very accurately assessed the state of digital photography, but management treated the study as, well, a snapshot rather than the beginning of a movie. Kodak ignored the fact that digital photography would keep improving at a furious pace throughout the 1980s, 1990s, and beyond.

Trouble also occurs when companies aren't open and transparent about what is certain and what is uncertain in the map they've laid out. When facts are mixed with conjecture, existing businesses can cast doubt on technologies that will clearly be disruptive and delay addressing them.

The problem is rarely lack of information. The problem is a lack of top-notch, hard-core expertise on how technology will unfold and be adopted. Think of the issue this way: Would a Fortune 1,000 organization have anyone other than one of the best finance professionals in the world as its chief financial officer? Few, however, have one of the 1,000 best computer scientists as chief information officer. To truly grasp your technology context and gain those 80 IQ points, you need to hire an expert in computer science. After all, it will do a lot to shape your future.

The second step in imagining the range of potential interactions is the focus of Rules 2 and 3, which are described below in detail. These rules will help you understand how you might be attacked and, even better, show you how to turn new capabilities into killer apps that will let you prosper.

~ *Rule 2*
Embrace Your Doomsday Scenario

On March 11, 2011, the worst earthquake and tsunami in Japan's modern history struck the Fukushima Daiichi nuclear power plant. The magnitude 9.0 earthquake was sixteen times as strong as the earthquake that the facility was designed to withstand. The tsunami was more than twice as high as the biggest wave contemplated during the facility's design. Yet the facility remained physically intact.

Here's the problem: Fukushima Daiichi was designed to withstand either an earthquake *or* a tsunami, not both at the same time, even though earthquakes can cause tsunamis. The earthquake knocked out the electrical power grid that supplied the facility, and the tsunami knocked out the on-site backup power generators. While the designers thought the site had fail-safe access to power, there was zero power for days. Even though the reactors automatically shut down, as designed, the cooling systems couldn't operate without power. The lack of cooling led to a cascade of other problems, resulting in severe damage and radioactive discharges.[39]

---

39 J. Buongiorno, R. Ballinger, M. Driscoll, B. Forget, C. Forsberg, M. Golay, M. Kazimi, N. Todreas, J. Yanch, "Technical Lessons Learned from the Fukushima-Daiichi Accident and Possible Corrective Actions for the Nuclear Industry: An Initial Evaluation," Massachusetts Institute of Technology, Center for Advanced Nuclear Energy Systems, May 2011, MIT-NSP-TR-025.

What played out at Fukushima Daiichi were the disastrous conse-quences of a failure of imagination. If the designers had considered the possibility of a simultaneous earthquake and tsunami, they might have produced a better design, without a lot of additional expense. For instance, the backup generators might have been elevated or located in waterproof enclosures, so they couldn't be knocked out by a tsunami. At minimum, disaster planning would have been better. Perhaps provi-sions would have been made for a ready supply of transportable gener-ators that could be brought to the site.

The approach taken at Fukushima Daiichi is common in the world of business. While executives may ask for a worst-case scenario, what they typically get is a kinda-bad-case scenario. If they push, they might get a really-bad-case scenario. But executives rarely face up to a true doomsday scenario.

They (you) must.

As late as 2010, even as it was racking up billions of dollars in losses, the US Postal Service was forecasting an *increase* in volume—this despite the blindingly obvious trend toward more electronic communication and less physical mail. The USPS actually gave its unions a no-layoffs clause in a contract signed in May 2011, only to break the contract a few months later and lay off 120,000 employees. The *pessimistic* scenario for first-class mail volume in 2017 was more than 10 percent higher than actual volume in 2013.[40]

Similarly, even after digital photography had started to savage Kodak's sales of film, chemicals, and photographic paper, the CEO assured investors in 2003 that the worst possible situation for the company would see it growing earnings by 8 percent a year. Instead, earnings turned into huge losses, and the company filed for bankruptcy protection in January 2012. To say that someone is "having a Kodak moment" no longer has the warm and fuzzy connotation it once did.

---

40   Mark Rogowsky, "First Class Mail Is Doomed. Get Over It," *Forbes*, February 15, 2013, http://www.forbes.com/sites/markrogowsky/2013/02/15/first-class-mail-is-doomed-get-over-it.

Looking forward, it's easy to see plenty of companies that need to contemplate doomsday. Television companies and cable operators, for example, spend a lot of time these days arguing that their business model is intact, that customers aren't going to "cut the cord" and switch to the Internet for their programming. Telecom companies have already adjusted to the disappearance of landlines in homes and are prepping for a gradual decline in voice revenues on mobile phones. But, what if they're all wrong and the change is precipitous? What if Google dramatically expands its Google Fiber program to support its ambitions in video (via YouTube) and mobile devices (via Motorola)? Google Fiber is already offering free basic Internet access in Kansas City and has announced plans to expand the offering into Austin, Texas, and Provo, Utah. While Google has been vague about its plans, it said recently that it sees fiber as a business, not just a demonstration. What if Microsoft takes advantage of its purchase of Skype by offering free telecom links as part of its defense of its Windows and Office software? Already, a cofounder of Skype has set up a business that gives away wireless bandwidth.[41] It's hard to compete with free.

But people are simply wired to avoid thinking about dire situations. No one wants to go around worrying about being struck by lightning. The tendency not to dwell on doomsday scenarios is fortified by the human propensity for unrealistic optimism. Fully 90 percent of drivers believe they are better than the average driver and therefore less likely to be involved in a serious accident.[42] Bad things might happen, we tell ourselves, but they happen to other people.

---

41   Ina Fried, "How Skype's Co-Founder Hopes to Make Money Giving Away Mobile Broadband," *All Things D,* March 22, 2012, http://allthingsd.com/20120322/how-skypes-co-founder-hopes-to-make-money-giving-away-mobile-broadband/?mod=tweet.

42   Shelley E. Taylor. *Positive Illusions: Creative Self-Deception and the Healthy Mind.* New York: Basic Books, 1989.

Businesses tend to be even more optimistic than individuals. Senior executives need to promise investors growth; talk of potential problems is such a downer. As executives move up the career ladder, they tend to believe their own PR—after all, only those who've been relentlessly successful keep moving up—so they think they can do just about anything. Underlings, hoping to move up that ladder themselves, know better than to try to make the bosses think about possible doomsdays. Many executives also have a bias toward action. They've seen too many ideas bog down in bureaucracy, so they become desperate to have an idea implemented, even if it's imperfect, and don't go looking for problems.

Besides, if problems develop, they usually happen long after those who laid the groundwork for them have moved on to bigger and better things. And executives are typically playing with OPM, which stands for Other People's Money and is pronounced, appropriately, like "opium." If ideas succeed, the executives get rich. If ideas fail, the investors are the big losers.

The problem is that doomsday scenarios do occur in business, and they occur much more frequently than executives are willing to acknowledge. We're not talking lightning strikes here.

Businesses need to understand their doomsday scenarios for three reasons. (And flat earnings for the next two quarters is not a doomsday scenario—bankruptcy, liquidation, and nuclear disaster are.)

The first reason is obvious: If you have a nuclear facility that's vulnerable to a natural disaster, you should know that. The other two reasons are encapsulated by a statement made by President Dwight Eisenhower: "Plans are worthless, but planning is everything." Looking at doomsday scenarios helps to build alignment, and it helps companies spot vulnerabilities and make improvements that will increase revenue and profits even if doomsday never comes.

Even if executive teams share a general view of looming threats, our experience is that they may differ greatly in their beliefs about how quickly those threats will arrive—without realizing their differences. In a project we did with a major publisher, for instance, executives all agreed that an important stream of print advertising revenue was going away soon because of the Internet. But it turned out that the team had wildly different views of what "soon" meant and therefore when compensating revenue streams or cost cuts were needed. This unstated disconnect led to executives working at cross-purposes, even though they thought they had alignment. An exercise based on alternate scenarios found that what some thought would happen in one year others thought wouldn't happen for five. With all the thoughts on the table, the group came to a consensus on timing and moved forward in unified fashion.

Because individuals and businesses aren't inclined to look at doomsday scenarios, and thus miss out on important analysis, executives must force themselves to go through the exercise periodically. Doomsday scenarios will rarely be considered in the normal course of business, so extra effort is required.

The best doomsday exercise is usually one we've dubbed Be Your Own Most Dangerous Competitor. In it, we divide managers into small groups and give them a simple charge: Imagine you get a call from an investor with plenty of capital who offers to finance a business that would put your current employer out of business and dominate the industry. You just have to come up with the right business plan. After considerable discussion, each team pitches its venture to the entire group, which then debates and votes on the best plan. Basically, we're asking the group to stare into the abyss and report what they see.

Freeing the participants from explicit and implicit organizational encumbrances often has a cathartic effect. They very much enjoy the exercise, and the discussion highlights dangerous weaknesses, untapped opportunities, and competitive challenges, while providing crisp interpretations of market trends. The exercise navigates past individual and group processes that stifle clear thinking and gives people a way to articulate what they know.

If you have trouble getting started, begin by brainstorming a list of events that might threaten your future—technology developments, customer activities, stakeholder actions, competitor actions, government actions, substitutions that might let new products or services supplant yours, and so on. Then plot each point on a chart where the x-axis is the "likelihood of occurrence" and the y-axis is the "importance to the business." Once the points are plotted, select events that have high likelihood and high importance. Assign teams to put each event into a coherent story and describe how such a scenario could come about within two or three years. Have each team present its scenario to the other teams, generating discussion that identifies some signposts to watch for.

AT&T shows the good that can come out of a doomsday exercise—as well as the perils of ignoring that discipline. The "good" AT&T goes all the way back to 1951. About forty leaders of Bell Labs, AT&T's renowned R&D laboratory, were ordered one night to clear their calendars for the next day and attend a meeting. The head of Bell Labs walked into the meeting and announced, "The telephone system of the United States was destroyed last night."

After considerable confusion, he conceded that, of course, the phone system had not been destroyed. But, for the purposes of the meeting, the executives should assume it had been. They were going to start a doomsday exercise that stretched over the next year.

Many of the most important contributions to the phone system of that time had been developed decades before. The dial, for example, was invented in the 1890s and introduced in the 1930s. The transatlantic cable connecting the United States and Great Britain was laid in 1882. The head of Bell Labs asked the meeting participants, with a straight face, "What the hell have you guys been doing? . . . You haven't improved the system a bit."

With that, he organized the group into teams charged with redesigning the entire phone system. Like most, the group assigned to redesign the telephone found itself wanting to ask what was wrong with the current telephone, then fix those problems. Instead, the group forced itself to ask what properties a telephone should have, if they were building one from scratch. The team came up with more than ninety desirable properties. Among them were "no wrong numbers," "knowing who was calling before answering the phone," and "not fixed but rather traveled with the user." Over the next year, the team established the technical feasibility of each design feature.

According to Russell Ackoff, a pioneer in management theory who participated in the project, the design teams anticipated almost every change in the telephone system for more than fifty years, except for the Internet and cameras in phones. Although AT&T didn't face anything like a doomsday for decades, it spotted vulnerabilities and migrated to crucial new capabilities.

We're not saying this one exercise sparked all the creativity within AT&T. In a place like Bell Labs, as in every large organization, innovations have multiple starting points. What the doomsday exercise did was to give coherence to many good ideas and provide a platform for them to find their way into the system. As Ackoff observed, "The impact of the design we produced was greater than the impact of any other effort to change a system that I had ever seen."[43]

---

43   Russell L. Ackoff, Jason Magidson, Herbert J. Addison, *Idealized Design: How to Dissolve Tomorrow's Crisis. . . Today,* New York, Pearson Prentice Hall, 2006.

By contrast, in 1964, Paul Baran, a researcher at Rand Corp. (as in, not AT&T), published a series of seminal papers that rethought the communications network from scratch. Baran offered a detailed design that was radically different from the analog, circuit-switched architecture of AT&T's communications network at the time. In a circuit-switched network, someone placing a call would have a circuit opened that would connect him to the recipient of the call. The bandwidth for that call would be reserved solely for that conversation for as long as the call lasted, even if neither party was talking. Baran's idea was, instead, to break every communication into tiny chunks, called packets. The packets would have a little address information attached to them that would say who, or what, the recipient of each packet was. The packets were sent individually, getting to the recipient through the most efficient path available. The packets were reassembled for the recipient, based on information attached to the packets that said what order they should be in.

Packet-switching may sound like an awful lot of work, and it takes a massive amount of computing, but it allows for a much more efficient network than a circuit-switched one. The ability to use multiple pathways means packets face few bottlenecks, and bandwidth doesn't lie idle when no one is talking. The proof? Packet-switching became the basis for the Internet, which never would have been possible using a circuit-switched network.

AT&T not only didn't foresee packet-switching; the company wanted "nothing to do with it," Baran said.[44] AT&T kept investing in its soon-to-be obsolescent approach. Robert Lucky, who ran a large part of Bell Labs in the 1980s and 1990s, told us that executives boasted that AT&T would dominate for years to come because it owned the nation's network of copper wires, and no one could afford to build a similar network. Shortly thereafter, Lucky said, AT&T wrote off the entire value of its network and had to build a packet-switched network from scratch.

---

44   Interview with Robert Lucky, a former senior executive at Bell Labs.

AT&T was again asleep at the, well, switch in the late 1990s. A colleague argued in our magazine *Context* that telecom companies needed to greatly accelerate the depreciation of their equipment. Based on Moore's Law about the exponential improvement in computing power, the column said telecom equipment should be depreciated by 50 percent every 1½ year to two years. Instead, telecom used straight-line depreciation over thirty years—writing down the value by 3 percent of the original price every year for three decades. The notion is silly on its face. Is any phone company really still using equipment that's thirty years old? Or even twenty? But AT&T and other telecom companies complained to us and stuck to their straight-line depreciation—then wrote off almost the entire value of their networks because new equipment had rendered the old equipment obsolete.

In other words, when AT&T would not imagine its doomsday scenario, the market turned the scenario into reality.

You'll be much better off if you anticipate the doomsday scenario.

~ *Rule 3*
Start with a Clean Sheet of Paper

Big companies often let their best assets become liabilities. Washington Mutual's performance in the subprime mortgage debacle shows how extraordinary a constraint profit can be. In 2005, CEO Kerry K. Killinger wrote to the bank's chief risk officer: "I have never seen such a high-risk housing market." A year later, Killinger wrote about "the speculative bubble." Yet Killinger kept *increasing* WaMu's exposure to housing. When panic began to hit the housing market in parts of the country in the summer of 2007, Killinger bragged that he had been right—and kept boosting his mortgage lending as fast as he could.[45] He was addicted to the short-term profits he could book on the mortgages. When the mortgage market seized up in 2008, WaMu became the biggest failure in the history of the American financial system. Killinger had seen the crash coming for years, but profits kept him from stepping out of the way.

Experience is a great asset, but it helps companies dominate old businesses, not new ones. How can anyone have experience at something that hasn't been done before? In fact, people experienced in doing things in old ways will bristle at change. Even doctors, who are exceptionally bright and research-oriented, have a hard time with new

---

45   Floyd Norris, "Eyes Open, WaMu Still Failed," *New York Times*, March 24, 2011, http://www.nytimes.com/2011/03/25/business/25norris.html?pagewanted=all.

techniques and technology. Studies have found that doctors tend to keep doing what they learned to do in medical school and in their residencies. It takes 15 years for established science to permeate medical practices, even for something as simple as having patients take an aspirin a day if they are at risk of heart attack.

Customer relationships are wonderful, too. Customers make the world go 'round. But, sometimes, the customers just want what they've always had and resist new products even if those products are going to be blockbusters. Kraft had a dominant position selling its Maxwell House coffee to grocery stores, which had no reason to want anything different. So it was Howard Schultz, not Kraft, who founded Starbucks and figured out how to sell $5 coffee drinks and made a fortune.

Plants, equipment, brands, partnerships—all of these can be liabilities, to name just a few.

The point is not to assume that inertia will keep you on top. As an incumbent, you wield great power, and you should win the future. But you have to recognize that your power can also be an anchor. You have to figure out how to tap into the power while gradually letting go of some current advantages so you can move to the assets that will be important for your future.

The factors that get in the way as market leaders try to innovate are both rational and, as our colleague Dan Ariely says, predictably irrational.

The rational side is explained by what Clayton Christensen calls "the innovator's dilemma." Market leaders are optimized to exploit their current success. Their success gives them a strong sense of what works, and what doesn't, under the current market conditions. Market leaders make good margins selling their existing products to their existing customers, and every dollar reinvested in those products generates a better return on investment than if those dollars are spent elsewhere.

That's worth repeating: It's hard to justify investment in real innovation when brand extensions or incremental improvements will make an existing product better, faster, or cheaper. Given a market leader's innovation dilemma, it's always rational in the short term, for example, for a movie studio to come out with a sequel, which is why we wind up with *Die Hard 5*. The movie studios can't help themselves. Sequels rarely make a ton of money, but they provide steady profit.

The irrational hurdles of a market leader's innovation dilemma are perhaps even more confounding. Success brings with it priorities to juggle, budgets to protect, bonuses to maximize, resources to defend, loyalties to reward, and egos to stroke. People have all sorts of incentives in big organizations to slow or halt innovation, and many manage to do so.

The rational and irrational pressures that stifle innovation are so strong that the only way to circumvent them is to step outside the normal business processes. It's not enough to simply be more aware or to try harder.

In our consulting work, we've had great success with an exercise we call Invent the Future. It helps clients achieve the best of both worlds: using all the assets that they've spent years or decades developing, while tapping into all the possibilities for innovation.

As with the doomsday scenario, we assemble a group of senior executives. We run them through exercises that culminate in their designing the ideal, next-generation form of their business. They don't just start with the existing business and think about how to improve it incrementally each quarter and each year, in the face of all the usual constraints. Instead, they start with a clean sheet of paper and think about key trends and looming inventions, then come up with the best ways they can imagine that everything could come together to transform the business. The executives are instructed to think without regard to the current state of the business and without worrying about what people, capabilities and other assets they would have to add or subtract to become that perfect version of their business.

As with the Be Your Own Most Dangerous Competitor exercise, the executives invariably enjoy the exercise and demonstrate impressive creativity. It seems everyone has a germ of an idea that would revolutionize a business. They just don't ordinarily get to voice that idea.

Some companies go through Invent the Future exercises as part of the occasional management retreat. Others make them part of the strategy-setting process and develop a detailed design over the course of months or even a year. Either way, starting with a clean sheet of paper is the best way to project an organization into a future that makes use of its assets in creative ways.

One caveat: When you start with a clean sheet of paper, don't settle for anything less than breakthroughs that could constitute killer apps. Don't waste time working on ideas that will be the equivalent of paving the cowpaths, to use an old line from the computer world. Focus on innovations that could be the equivalent of superhighways or, better yet, the jet airplane.

We coined the name for the Invent the Future approach because of our friend and colleague Alan Kay, who famously said, "The best way to predict the future is to invent it." Kay was the catalyst for one of the best examples of using a clean sheet: He predicted Apple's invention of the iPad almost twenty years before it happened.

In 1986, Kay went to Apple CEO John Sculley and said, "Next time, we won't have Xerox." Kay, an Apple fellow at the time, was referring to the fact that the main components of Apple's desktop publishing system all sprang from inventions at Xerox PARC. Without Xerox to provide a template, what would drive Apple's vision?

As Sculley tells the story,[46] Kay said that every innovative technology, no matter how simple or how complex, takes fifteen to twenty years to evolve from concept to a commercial state.[47] If this were true, then many technologies important to Apple's future were already

---

46   Ian Piumarta and Kimberly Rose, eds. *Points of View: A Tribute to Alan Kay.* Viewpoints Research Institute, May 2010.

47   Because technology has faster cycle times these days, that fifteen- to twenty-year lead time has shrunk considerably.

percolating their way through the process. Kay, Sculley, and others spent the next year assessing the best ideas in computing and mapping out a twenty-year vision that came to be called Knowledge Navigator. It didn't just assume a huge increase in processing power but imagined what users would do with that power. The Knowledge Navigator was basically an iPad.

Soon after the vision of the Knowledge Navigator was pulled together, a team of Apple technologists and marketing pros produced a video depicting a Berkeley professor working in a home office in 2009.[48] Watching the video today, it's impossible to miss the conceptual predecessors of Siri, FaceTime, iCloud, multi-touch displays, embedded cameras, gesture and voice controls, and other distinctive elements of the iPad. It's also hard not to marvel that the iPad was introduced less than five months after the timeframe posited in the video.

All the capabilities sound elementary now, but they were a reach in 1987. Computers at that point were so slow that video overpowered them. Screens were black and white. A user had access to the information on his hard drive, but that was about it—in fact, many computers still only had floppy drives. While Macs had the sort of graphical interface and windows we've all come to expect, those were in rudimentary form, and so-called Wintel PCs (for Windows/Intel) still required users to type in arcane commands at the "C prompt." A big issue was how to improve "computer literacy," because the silly things were so hard to use.

In its time, the Knowledge Navigator was a sensation. Sculley used it as a way to keep Apple in front of the world as a culture rich with innovation and creativity. Mainstream media hailed it as visionary. It was shown at internal meetings to rally Apple employees. And for a time, at least, it protected Apple's lead in its core education markets.

---

48   "Apple Knowledge Navigator—1988," October 18, 2011, http://www.youtube.com/watch?v=xp4aRpcX5So&feature=player_embedded.

Apple had drawn on its assets in 1987, including brilliant folks such as Kay, but had designed a future that had almost nothing to do with the Macintosh business that dominated at the time. Then, Apple gradually worked its way to its idealized future.

While the Knowledge Navigator was unusually prescient, it wasn't science fiction. This wasn't Jules Verne taking people to the center of the Earth. Sculley says Kay was convinced that the Knowledge Navigator was a plausible view of the future, though Sculley marvels that Kay could see in 1987 what wasn't apparent to the rest of us until twenty-some years later—another argument for hiring world-class computer scientists.

Apple formed a joint venture with Acorn Computers and VLSI in 1990 that ultimately contributed very directly to the success of the iPad. The joint venture, ARM Holdings, designed chips specifically for mobile devices such as the Knowledge Navigator. As a result, ARM's chips cost a small fraction of Intel's general-purpose processors and have far lower power consumption than the chips Intel has produced to date, thus providing much longer charges on a battery.[49] Apple used the Knowledge Navigator as a guiding principle in its R&D labs even after Sculley left Apple in 1993. When Steve Jobs returned to the helm in 1997, the work was waiting for him. He eventually worked his magic on the technology and, using ARM chips, released the iPad to acclaim in 2010.

MIT provides a more current example of what can be accomplished with a clean sheet of paper. Perhaps because MIT lives on the cutting edge of technology—among many other things, the e-ink used in Amazon's Kindle came out of the MIT Media Lab—the university moved into online education very early. While many universities hold to the notion that the old ways are best or maybe consider ways to slowly

---

49   Intel didn't start with a clean sheet of paper, working instead from existing designs. In 2013, the company finally released low-power chips that some analysts believe will help it succeed in the mobile market, but it has paid a heavy price over the past decade for believing it could avoid starting fresh.

modify the centuries-old approach to higher education, MIT started from scratch and imagined a world that was some optimal combination of in-person instruction and labs, augmented by rich online video of lectures, demonstrations, and simulations.

While the right combination was initially unclear, and while MIT is still testing its way toward the right answer, MIT got started back in 2002, posting course materials for more than 2,000 courses on the Internet, for anyone to access. In late 2011, MIT began offering instruction online, to its students and others, as part of what it called MITx. It hoped for about ten times as many students as took the regular course on circuits and electronics, which would have meant about 1,500 students. In fact, in just the first few hours, 10,000 people signed up from around the world. More than 155,000 eventually signed up for the first course. In the spring of 2012, MIT joined forces with Harvard and founded edX. Each pumped $30 million into the nonprofit venture. Numerous universities have since signed on to offer instruction through the edX platform, including Stanford, Wellesley, Georgetown, Rice, and the University of Texas. As of this writing, more than 900,000 people have signed up for edX courses, and more than 31,000 have earned passing grades.[50]

Plenty of hurdles remain. For instance, faculty at many universities will surely fight what are being called MOOCs (massive open online courses). Amherst faculty recently voted against participation in edX. Philosophy professors at San Jose State University sent a letter saying they would not use the edX version of a Harvard professor's famous introductory class on social justice.

Even if faculty go along with MOOCs, many issues have to be worked out. While people sign up in vast numbers, only a small percentage complete the course—the highest percentage yet recorded for any MOOC is a 19 percent completion rate, and the average is about

---

50   Nathan Heller, "Laptop U," *New Yorker*, May 20, 2013, http://www.newyorker.com/reporting/2013/05/20/130520fa_fact_heller?currentPage=all&utm_source=EdsurgeLive&utm_campaign=4d3d7e95c0-2013_05_08_EdSurge_Newsletter_Ver_1175_7_2013&utm_medium=email&utm_term=0_0f1ec25b60-4d3d7e95c0-266758717.

7 percent.[51] Issues also have to be resolved about how to provide credit for the MOOCs and how, perhaps, to integrate those into the granting of college degrees. People will have to work out the right formats, figure out intellectual property rights (if a professor who teaches a MOOC leaves, does it leave with her or stay with the university?), and figure out how much to charge.

Still, MOOCs show real potential. At San Jose State University, an engineering class that blended edX material with the traditional approach saw the pass rate reach 91 percent, versus the historical average of 59 percent. The state of California announced that San Jose State will offer MOOCs that provide remedial education in subjects such as math, where many students are deficient upon entering college. The courses will cost just $150 each.[52] (The project was later put on hold to get the kinks worked out.) While even supporters of MOOCs acknowledge the benefits of having world-class professors interact face-to-face with students, a small percentage of students get that opportunity at elite universities, so MOOCs could do a lot to improve the education of those who attend junior colleges, community colleges, and technical schools.

Interestingly, at a time when the United States is concerned about a lack of training in STEM (science, technology, engineering, and mathematics), MOOCs could radically change the economics of such education—in fact, in May 2013, Georgia Tech announced plans to offer a master's degree in computer science that will cost students a grand total of $7,000. Historically, STEM education has been expensive because of all the lab work, demonstrations, and simulations, while education in the humanities has been cheap—all you need is a professor with a tweed jacket with patches on the elbows, plus a book and a conference table. With MOOCs, though, the demonstrations and

---

51   Ibid.

52   Ibid.

simulations can be done once, and grading is easy because answers in technical fields are cut and dried. In the humanities, however, judgments are subjective, and it will be much more time-consuming to provide feedback to students taking MOOCs.

From the standpoint of MIT, things are still very confusing, but however the situation shakes out, MIT will be in the thick of things. Its willingness to take out a clean sheet of paper and invent some possible futures means the university is learning as much and as fast as any potential competitor.

Walgreens provides another good example of the power of rethinking from scratch. The pharmacy chain didn't start especially early, unlike MIT, but it's making up for lost time and claiming a new position in health care as the world of medicine is reinvented.

Like many iconic businesses, Walgreens started with a fundamental reconception—but that was a long time ago, not long after Charles Walgreen moved to Chicago in 1893 at age twenty and, in a gesture symbolic of a fresh start, took the last pennies out of his pocket and threw them into the river. After working in a pharmacy for close to a decade, Walgreen bought a drugstore on the South Side and revolutionized the concept. He widened the aisles, improved lighting, and broadened the selection, including pots and pans. He emphasized personal service—and was clever about making sure customers noticed. When someone called in a prescription, Walgreen said it loudly and distinctly so an assistant could fill it while Walgreen stayed on the phone. Walgreen would chat up the caller to keep her on the phone long enough for the assistant to arrive with the prescription—customers talked about how Walgreen was so fast he'd deliver your order before you could even hang up the phone. Going beyond soda fountains, whose cold concoctions were popular only during summer, Walgreen installed a lunch counter that stayed busy year-round.[53] (During Prohibition, his pharmacies were known to stock whisky

---

53   Terry Hogan, "Backtracking: Charles R. Walgreen, One of Galesburg's Own," *Galesburg Zephyr,* http://www.thezephyr.com/backtrack/cwalgreen.htm.

behind the counter.) By 1929, the one Walgreens store had turned into 525. Two generations later, in 2000, after a grandson turned Walgreens into the iconic corner drugstore, the company operated more than 8,000 stores across the United States.[54]

But there weren't many more corners to occupy, so expansion needed to slow. Meanwhile, pressure was building, partly because of the Internet. Huge intermediaries known as pharmacy benefits managers (PBMs) had sprung up to negotiate better prices for corporate insurance plans, and the PBMs were squeezing profits out of pharmacies such as Walgreens. The PBMs helped steer customers toward mail order and the Internet for medicines that they needed to order repeatedly, rather than going to their local drugstores. Roughly two-thirds of Walgreens's sales comes from filling prescriptions, so online defections stung.[55] At the same time, the spread of other types of convenience stores, including those at gas stations, cut into other sales.

Rather than fight a defensive war of attrition, in 2006 Walgreens took out a clean sheet of paper. Executives had seen competitors open clinics and realized that Walgreens might be able to skim off a layer of health care that hospitals didn't provide efficiently, undercutting them on cost while bringing more traffic into stores. Walgreens started small, with mostly nurse practitioners treating pink eye and strep throat and administering flu shots. But, finding customers receptive to low prices and short waits, Walgreens has steadily offered more complicated procedures. In 2007, Walgreens bought Take Care Health Systems, which has 700 clinics across the country, and began treating chronic diseases such as diabetes, hypertension, high cholesterol, and

---

54   "Former Walgreen Co. Chairman Charles R. Walgreen Jr. Dies At 100," Walgreens.com, February 11, 2007, http://news.walgreens.com/article_print. cfm?article_id=2822.

55   "Walgreen Taps Prescription Sales and Retail Clinic Demand for Growth," *Seeking Alpha,* April 11, 2013, http://seekingalpha.com/article/1335801-walgreen-taps-prescription-sales-and-retail-clinic-demand-for-growth.

asthma.[56] Walgreens also provides certain kinds of care in homes and assisted-living facilities, and has announced plans to provide hospice care nationally. Basically, Walgreens has imagined itself a role as the nurse practitioner of the United States, leveraging its brand and its 8,500 locations around the country. As PBMs and others eat away at the company's prescription business, Walgreens is moving upstream and stealing business from hospitals and other health care providers.

Microsoft serves as the object lesson on what happens if you don't start with a clean sheet of paper. Microsoft has virtually owned the market for operating systems on personal computers for almost three decades and dominates the market for applications. Microsoft's central role in the world of personal computing has meant that it has access to virtually every customer and has given it leverage that competitors simply couldn't withstand. Yet, because Microsoft has taken an incremental approach to progress, constrained by its prior success, the company has missed a remarkable string of opportunities for innovation.

The missed opportunities include search engines like Google, digital music systems like the iPod and iTunes, e-book readers like the Kindle, smartphones like the iPhone and those based on the Android operating system,[57] tablets like the iPad, and social media platforms like Facebook and Twitter. All of these are spokes on the personal computing hub that Microsoft dominates, so Microsoft should have had an advantage in launching them.

---

56 Brigid Sweeney, "Drugstore Drama: The Old Ways No Longer Work for Walgreen," *Crain's Chicago Business*, July 18, 2011, http://www.chicagobusiness.com/article/20110716/ISSUE01/307169974/drugstore-drama-the-old-ways-no-longer-work-for-walgreen#ixzz2TPAa5ym8.

57 Microsoft's share of smartphone subscribers in the United States was 36 percent in 2007, when the iPhone was introduced, but that percentage had fallen to 4 percent by spring 2012. Dan Frommer, "Microsoft's Mobile Comeback Is Looking Terrible," *Business Insider*, April 24, 2012, http://articles.businessinsider.com/2012-04-24/tech/31390913_1_windows-phones-smartphone-market-iphone.

It's not that Microsoft didn't see the opportunities. In fact, Microsoft spends nearly $10 billion a year on R&D[58] and invested heavily in pursuit of most of these new product areas. Instead, the main problem was that Microsoft's existing businesses got in the way of future ones. For instance, while Microsoft saw the potential for tablets early on and announced a major development effort, the company's dominant Office group sabotaged the effort by refusing to let Office applications work properly on the tablet. As it happens, Microsoft gave up on tablets just months before Apple introduced the iPad. While Microsoft couldn't get even a reasonable product to market, Apple sold 300,000 iPads on April 3, 2010, the very first day it was available. Apple went on to sell almost 15 million units in 2010. Microsoft also began developing an e-reader in 1997, inspired by Douglas Adams's *Hitchhiker's Guide to the Galaxy,* which described a book that could hold all the knowledge in the galaxy. Though Microsoft began its work almost a decade before Amazon brought its Kindle to market, executives resisted the e-reader because its interface didn't look enough like Windows—nevermind that people wanted a book to look like a book, not like a PC, and wanted to be able to touch the screen with a finger, not use a stylus or keyboard. The developers initially hoped to bring out a product in 2003 or 2004 but were quickly moved into an operating division and told they needed to turn a profit. The developers rushed a product to market in 1999, to run on the Microsoft Pocket PC, a phone-size device with a tiny screen. A version for Windows followed. The e-reader flopped.[59,60]

58   Kevin L. Jackson, "Cloud to Command 90% of Microsoft's R&D Budget," *Forbes,* April 19, 2011, http://www.forbes.com/sites/kevinjackson/2011/04/19/cloud-to-command-90-of-microsofts-rd-budget/.

59   Kurt Eichenwald, "Microsoft's Lost Decade," *Vanity Fair,* August 2012, http://www.vanityfair.com/business/2012/08/microsoft-lost-mojo-steve-ballmer.

60   Dick Brass, "Microsoft's Creative Destruction," *New York Times,* February 4, 2010, http://www.nytimes.com/2010/02/04/opinion/04brass.html?pagewanted=all.

Microsoft defends its work over the past decade, noting that revenue has tripled since 2000 and that it has been a cash-generating machine.[61] But the stock price tells the real story. Stock prices reflect the value of all the cash flow a company is expected to generate in the future, and Microsoft's stock price has been essentially flat since 2000. That means Microsoft just harvested the opportunities that had already been created and that investors recognized in 2000. While Apple, MIT, and Walgreens used a clean sheet of paper, Microsoft whiffed on the whole host of easy opportunities it had to invent a different future—and CEO Steve Ballmer announced in August 2013 that he would retire early.

Microsoft is now on the defensive. It's fighting to preserve its PC operating system in a world that's rapidly moving away from PCs. Microsoft is also defending its suite of Office products at a time when Google's free alternatives are gaining mainstream acceptance.

Kay recently told us a variant of his famous invent-the-future line that applies to companies that cling to existing businesses and decline to reinvent themselves. At those companies, Kay says, the view is that "the best way to predict the future is to prevent it."

---

61   Rich Karlgaard, "Microsoft's Steve Ballmer Talks about Windows 8, Bill Gates and Steve Jobs—and Why Microsoft's Lost Decade Is a Myth," *Forbes*, July 11, 2012, http://www.forbes.com/sites/richkarlgaard/2012/07/11/microsofts-steve-ballmer-talks-about-windows-8-bill-gates-and-steve-jobs-and-why-microsofts-lost-decade-is-a-myth/2/.

~ *Case Study*
Carmakers Must Take a New Road

In 2008, when Facebook was still a toddler, Google's then-CEO Eric Schmidt started writing memos about the impressive prospects for social media—but neither he nor others in Google's leadership made social networking a priority. Schmidt said the failure to follow through was the biggest mistake of his ten-year tenure: "I clearly knew that I had to do something, and I failed to do it. I screwed up." [62]

But business is a world of batting averages, and Google's batting average has been very high when it comes to thinking big. For instance, when it comes to identifying trends in technology, Google embraced mobile very early and publicly. Schmidt said years ago that everyone would be on mobile devices, even though Google's business at the time was based on search on PCs and even though the company didn't yet have a business model for the mobile world. Schmidt meant what he said, too: Google went out and bought Android so it would have an operating system for mobile phones, made early deals with Apple to get maps and YouTube on the iPhone, and so on.

---

62   John Paczkowski, "Schmidt Says Google's Social Networking Problem Is His Fault," *All Things D,* May 31, 2011, http://allthingsd.com/20110531/world-would-benefit-from-facebook-alternative-says-google-chairman/.

Google has also, based on its actions, done a seemingly stellar job of imagining doomsday scenarios. Google imagined a world where Apple controls the entire ecosystem for mobile devices, where people buy everything through Amazon without having to first search for the best prices and features on Google, where people use Facebook as their starting point for the Internet rather than go through Google's search engine, where Microsoft uses brute force to maintain control of individuals' computing experience, and so on. The game of four-dimensional chess is still playing out, so Google could still lose, but the company has thus far done an impressive job of responding to all the existential threats.

Google has also done a good job of using clean sheets of paper. It set up the Google X lab, which reportedly has one hundred projects going and which has produced such innovative prototypes as the driverless car and Google Glass. More recently, it went even further and launched a program called Solve for X, where X is a remedy to some broad problem and where the projects, referred to as moonshots, are even more ambitious than those in the Google X lab. It isn't always clear from the outside what the various innovation projects have to do with Google's core business. But the projects have at least some connection to the Google goal of organizing the world's information—and many could be transformative.

If carmakers are going to win the coming round of breakthrough innovation, competing against Google and many others, they'll have to do nearly as good a job of thinking big as Google has.

That will be difficult. Many went through near-death experiences in the Great Recession and surely don't want to contemplate more. The carmakers feel like they've solved their biggest problems, related to union contracts and debt. In general, executives have been arguing for some time that they've been changing as fast as they can (even if that often wasn't fast enough). Now that many trends are favorable, why go looking for trouble? Wouldn't it be nice to think small for a while?

Traditional car companies also must overcome their cultures and their business models. Automakers are filled with "car guys." Even the women are car guys. Car guys love cars and the thrill of driving. Some still have a difficult time accepting automatic transmissions, anti-lock brakes, and cruise control. Imagine their emotional reaction to *not driving*. The car-guy mindset is so strong that it could limit the possibilities for innovation that the incumbents consider. The business model also limits carmakers' ability to pursue potentially important ideas for innovation because what company would try to invent a future that included 90 percent fewer cars?

Organizational structure may be an issue, too. Companies that, like the carmakers, have a strong central organization or that are organized by function tend to have rigid processes and emphasize efficient operations. Such companies tend to keep doing what they've always done, just a little better each quarter, rather than looking for breakthroughs.

As a result, car companies may strive for incremental improvement. General Motors, for instance, prepared a video that described self-driving and accident-prevention technology as "enhancements to the driving experience" and "the next stage in that evolution."[63] Self-driving technology may, in fact, ultimately be adopted incrementally, but assuming an incremental approach will be very limiting in these early stages of innovation.

Carmakers will be tempted to dismiss Google's efforts as pie in the sky. The car companies know who their competitors are, they believe, after decades of going at each other, hammer and tongs—plus socket wrenches and industrial robots. Besides, Google doesn't even make any physical products. It just produces software and deals in information and online ads. Google may have plenty of intellectual horsepower,

---

63   World Car Fans, "Cadillac Semi-Autonomous Driving," April 20, 2012, http://
www.youtube.com/watch?v=Op2Qj3tG2aQ.

but there's no vroom, vroom to what Google does. Far from being car guys, Google distributes old-style bicycles around its campus in Mountain View, California, for employees to grab at will and ride to other buildings.

But Google is the kind of diagonal competitor that all the companies in the car industry need to take seriously. It doesn't have to supplant the carmakers, for instance, to win. If its driverless car succeeds, Google could provide a sort of operating system for autos, no matter the manufacturer. That operating-system thing worked great for Microsoft, while the companies that actually made PCs struggled to make any kind of profit. Success by Google could turn carmakers into the equivalent of Foxconn, which makes Apple products but gets a teensy share of the earnings. (Similar "operating systems" could appear in many other industries through innovations such as mobile payments and ads and electronic health records.)

As we've said, we believe the advantage lies with the major players, in this case the GMs and Fords of the world. They know way more about cars than Google does, and they have the brands, the networks of dealers, and so on. But they'll have to figure out creative ways to build on those assets while avoiding many pitfalls. They have to set aside their propensity to, say, not look at innovation that might slash the number of cars on the road. The established players also have to consider such heretical possibilities as developing technology that, like the Google driverless-car software, could be used across the industry and not just provide a way to sell more Cadillacs or Audis.

Taking a broad look isn't simple. Strong cultures tend to put a pillow over disruptive ideas and smother them before they get big enough to defend themselves. History provides a depressing array of examples of companies that failed to adapt to a major shift.

To avoid the same fate, and take advantage of the unprecedented opportunities out there, carmakers will have to make sure they Think Big, beginning with the technology context.

Let's look at some applications for each of the six technology megatrends:

- **Mobile devices.** Cars are the ultimate mobile computing devices. It's possible to imagine them as almost any sort of computer, whether using built-in screens or screens that people bring into the car with them. Cars could become Wi-Fi hubs or even cooperate with other cars and form a mesh network, providing free, high-speed access to the Internet to cars and to passengers. It's important to think of cars as nodes in a larger network, interacting with other information networks, apps, and resources, some of which customers carry with them and some of which are accessed over the Internet. We expect, for example, that future cars' customer-satisfaction ratings with depend as much on how well software apps run in them as on how well the cars themselves run.

- **Social media.** Driving is no longer a solitary experience. Technology is changing it into a social one, as demonstrated by the number of drivers who insist on phoning and texting while driving—in spite of research showing the danger of doing so. So, clearly, social (and, we hope, safe) mobile apps will be high on drivers' wish lists. Social media will also greatly influence which cars people buy, and even whether people buy cars— studies have found that young people drive less than previous generations because they can meet up with friends online and no longer need to drive places.

- **Cameras.** Cameras will be everywhere—in cars, at intersections, on buildings, and on roadsides—to monitor traffic. Carmakers and their partners will use them to enhance the safety of drivers and passengers;

already, many cars have cameras that turn on when someone is backing up and let the driver see what's behind her, helping avoid accidents. Cameras monitoring traffic will be used to knit cars together into a true network. The only limitation will be privacy concerns; people get twitchy if they think Big Brother is always watching. Cameras will change how people drive.

- **Sensors.** Like cameras, sensors will be ubiquitous. It will no longer be necessary to make a cut in a road to add sensors that communicate with traffic lights; cars themselves or the phones inside them will talk to the lights and, through them, to traffic management systems. It will be possible to monitor in real time all aspects of a car's performance, the driver's performance, and the flow of traffic. Already, sensors mounted on street lights are spotting empty parking spaces in cities and transmitting the information to a central system, which can alert drivers. Again, the only limits will stem from privacy concerns.

- **Cloud computing.** Some computing will be done in cars, but much of it will move to the cloud, working from new information about maps, weather, traffic, similar cars, and so on. Rather than remain unchanged from the day it's purchased, a car will receive software updates just as personal computing devices do and will tap into whatever up-to-the-second information is needed.

- **Emergent knowledge.** Manufacturers will know just about everything about how their cars are being used, how the vehicle as a whole and individual parts perform, and so on. Manufacturers might also learn quite a bit about competitors if, say, cities decide to raise funds by selling access to the video feeds at intersections. Car design will improve. Drivers will learn how they compare with others and will be able to adjust their behavior; no longer will 90 percent be able to claim that they're above average. And, as demonstrated by the Google car, artificial intelligence techniques will translate new data feeds into better tools for driving, both in support of, and in place of, the human driver. The list of possible types of new knowledge could go on and on.

- **All of the above.** Taken together, these six technologies will transform how cars are designed and used, and how society organizes itself around them.

Among the many near-term possibilities that could emerge are black boxes that record what happens right before a car crashes, just as black boxes in airplanes do. Rudimentary forms of these already exist in many cars because laws mandating airbags included provisions designed to monitor what triggered them, but very sophisticated monitoring and recording devices are now possible at minimal cost. These black boxes could provide information about how cars react in crashes that would go far beyond what is learned in controlled tests with crash dummies. The boxes would, at the same time, simplify issues for police, remove the need for many personal-injury lawyers, cut into insurance fraud by those faking injuries, and much more. (The video from head-cams worn by many cyclists is already being used to find hit-and-run drivers or to sort out blame when a cyclist and car collide.)

Combining sensors and cameras in the cloud could provide enough emergent knowledge that traffic management would become much more efficient, reducing the need for road construction. Over time, it will be possible to think about cars as an always-connected platform for many applications and activities for drivers (if we need them) and passengers as they move from one place to another, rather than just as a tool for transportation. It also makes sense to think of managing cars as a network, rather than as hundreds of millions of individual things.

Once carmakers have started to lay out their technology context, they'll need to think about doomsday scenarios—and there are many. Perhaps the most dramatic challenge posed to automakers would come if driverless technology enabled massive car sharing. Most cars sit unused 95 percent of the time. If cars could autonomously move from one passenger to the next, the increased utilization could dramatically reduce costs. A study at Columbia University's Earth Institute found, for example, that car sharing could reduce the cost per trip-mile by as much as 80 to 90 percent.[64] This would result in significant threats to automakers' current business models.

First, according to Larry Burns, former head of research, development, and strategic planning at General Motors, fleet-level car sharing would change the composition of the cars that automakers could sell. His reasoning goes like this: Car sharing allows for the matching of vehicles to each particular trip. Because most car trips are short and involve one or two people, most cars in a shared fleet could be smaller, simpler, and cheaper electric vehicles. Rather than benefiting from customers' buying based on their worst-case scenario—the longest trip they might take, with the largest number of kids in the soccer carpool—carmakers might have to deal with fleet operators mostly buying commodity vehicles.

Such commodity cars would erode already thin profit margins and undercut business models that depend on the allure of premium autos and on options that carry large profit margins. Simplicity in cars would also reduce the traditional competitive advantages that stem from

64 "Transforming Personal Mobility," Lawrence D. Burns, William C. Jordan, and Bonnie A. Scarborough, Earth Institute, Columbia University, January 27, 2013.

automakers' ability to manage complex supply chains and integrate thousands of parts. Simpler cars would likewise reduce the necessary engineering expertise and capital costs, two barriers to entry that have protected automakers from new entrants.

Car sharing would also greatly accelerate product cycles. If all our driving is crammed into 10 or even 50 percent fewer cars, those cars will be used up and replaced much faster. Rather than having the population of cars turn over about every 15 years, the population would turn over every couple of years. Cars would become much more of a hits-based business, and it would be crucial not to miss a product cycle— look at what happened to Nokia and BlackBerry when they missed a cycle in cell phones.

What if Google extends the cell phone analogy and starts practically giving cars away to those willing to sign a multiyear contract for connectivity or using Google's software in the car? The subsidies might be worth it to Google because of the money it could make by having people use its search capabilities, maps, and business software in their cars. How does a carmaker compete with free or almost free?

There are plenty of other possible doomsday scenarios, too, based on developments with electric cars, regulation, and competitors. What happens, for instance, if the emerging middle class in China somehow generates the modern-day equivalent of the Volkswagen Beetle and sweeps through the US market?

The right scenarios to worry about are embedded in the heads of the carmakers' executive teams; it's up to those teams to give voice to their worst fears based on the sort of doomsday exercise we've laid out.

The conversation should resemble one that a colleague of ours at the Devil's Advocate Group, Vincent Barabba, led GM's senior management through in the early 2000s. He laid out several doomsday scenarios, including the possibility that environmental concerns would cause consumers to reject internal-combustion engines.

That'll never happen, he was told. But, rather than let the group simply move on, a GM executive vice president, Harry Pearce, suggested a more palatable version of the scenario. He asked the group to assume that one of GM's most respected scientists had proved that CO_2 emissions from vehicles using fossil-based fuels were the primary cause of global warming. Pearce said GM would have to act. Once everyone caught the spirit of the process, they realized that the current long-term plan would leave GM vulnerable to competitors that were working on alternatives to internal-combustion engines, as well as to possible government intervention.

Rick Wagoner, the CEO at the time, decided it would be prudent to restart research and development efforts into electric cars. While the internal-combustion engine didn't go away, the R&D produced advances in hybrid propulsion, fuel cells, and clean fuels that enabled GM to respond quickly when gas prices soared some years later. GM accelerated its work and came out with the hybrid Volt in 2011. The Volt generated some buzz: *Motor Trend* magazine named it the "car of the year" for 2011, labeling it a symbol of the "new GM" and a "game-changer." Sales have been disappointing, and the jury is still out about whether Volt will ever amount to much, but GM is surely glad that it stared into the abyss and considered life without the engine that has sustained the industry for more than a century.

Once the carmakers play defense and consider their dooms, they'll need to switch to offense and get out a clean sheet of paper. Carmakers have long complained that they do all the complex manufacturing for meager margins while downstream players make all the money, on financing, service, and insurance. Rather than continue with their traditional business model, built around supplying cars to car dealers, automakers could explore business models where they move downstream and engage more directly with consumers. For instance, they might conceive of themselves as a concierge service around the maintenance of the car and other kinds of activities that customers associate with driving. They might provide, for a fee, remote changes to engine settings that provide more horsepower or more efficiency for someone about to drive into the mountains; collect information on car performance, interpret it and feed it back to the customer; or help coordinate any service or repairs—in other words, put themselves smack in the middle of all the value in the car market.

To blunt the rise of car-sharing fleets, automakers might enhance the attraction of car ownership by helping individual car owners make extra money by renting their unused cars to strangers. That's what General Motors is doing in partnership with RelayRides, a company that facilitates peer-to-peer car sharing, in which car owners rent their cars by the hour. Using OnStar, GM lets drivers unlock cars using their smartphones, eliminating the hassle of exchanging keys in person.

Automakers could even become fleet operators themselves. Rather than being in the car business, they could move into car-focused transportation. Automakers might lease cars by the mile.

Carmakers could imagine a world with far fewer dealers, where people can go, see, and test-drive cars, then order them directly from the manufacturer. Perhaps, the manufacturers would conceive of dealerships as like Apple stores: hip places where people would visit frequently to buy the latest cool apps for their cars.

Maybe companies would reconceive cars as a platform like iPhones and let third parties create apps that could be sold through something akin to the App Store. A friend of ours who works at a big car company offered some possibilities based on bits of software he's written using his access to the company's application programming interfaces. He has his car text his wife when he's 10 minutes from home. (He did once cause some confusion when he went out of town and lent his car to a friend who lived nearby. As the man returned home from work, to a house a few streets over from our friend's, the car dutifully texted our friend's wife. Confused, she called our friend and said, "What's going on? I thought you were out of town.") When his teenage daughter takes his car out at night, he has it give her a 10-minute warning, based on her location, about when she'll have to leave to make it home before her curfew; he says the notification makes her feel more secure. He says an electric car could be programmed so that it would draw power only when rates fell below a certain level. He's thinking of having his wife's car text him when it's down to a quarter-tank, so he can fill it up.

A carmaker could also take, say, a ten-year view and imagine a world of driverless cars. That view might involve producing a sort of operating system that would outdo Google's and put the car company in control. The company might also develop scenarios where it would be in the carmaker's interest to accelerate the adoption of driverless cars, rather than push back against them to defend existing territory. Again, the implementation issues would wait until after the ideal was laid out. Only when the future businesses were envisioned would the team be allowed to think about the expenses that would come with closing dealerships, the laws that protect dealers' relationships with customers, and so on.

With potential death threats and killer opportunities defined, the carmaker could then turn to the next step in our process: Start Small. That means following rules that give innovative ideas a true test and a chance to take hold within a big business, but without spending a potentially crippling amount of money.

PHASE TWO: START SMALL

~ Rule 4
First, Let's Kill All the Finance Guys

Yes, the classic line from Shakespeare's *Henry VI, Part Two* is, "The first thing we do, let's kill all the lawyers," not, "Let's kill all the finance guys." We both have loved ones who are lawyers, so we enjoy a joke about wiping out lawyers as much as the next person. (Q: What do you call a thousand lawyers, chained together at the bottom of the ocean? A: A good start.) But when it comes to innovating in business, the fine folks in finance are most often the ones who unintentionally distort the innovation process. Some way—short of bodily harm—needs to be found to limit their involvement during the early stages of innovation.

Nobody intends harm, of course, but the methods that finance uses can have two devastating effects on big ideas.

The most common problem is that innovations are held up to unfair standards. The best finance departments have sophisticated processes that govern the margin requirements, planning windows, size thresholds, and so on, for projects that deserve corporate resources. But it's almost impossible for big, long-term, uncertain innovation ideas to pass the short-term tests that are applied to an existing business—even when it's clear that the existing business is under threat and that the business itself won't meet traditional standards for long, either.

Sears shows the pitfalls when finance imposes its will on innovation too soon. Hedge fund manager Edward S. Lampert bought Sears in 2005 for $11 billion, fresh off a killing at Kmart, and was hailed as the next Warren Buffett.[65] He had impeccable credentials in finance and a string of successes, mostly notably at Auto Nation. He vowed to return Sears to its preeminent place in American retailing. But, it seems, no innovation ever made it past Lampert's financial screens—not ads, not new store formats, nothing. So, he spent extremely little money even when an idea was promising. He ended up with stores that reminded some of those in the Eastern bloc.

This is what happened when Lampert converted a Kmart into a Sears Essentials, which he had described as a bold new concept:

"Sears Essentials flopped. It was not because Kmart shoppers rejected Sears products, but because the experiment seemed to consist only of tossing Kenmore stoves and Craftsman hammers into an old Kmart store, rather than creating a vibrant new shopping experience.

"The former Kmart in Parsippany, NJ...sits in a bustling suburban shopping center, surrounded by popular retailers. ...[But] a visitor found mismatched floor tiles in the lobby, Reagan-era beige shelves in the food aisles and a ragged brown carpet in the clothing department. Near a customer service desk, a broken pipe dripped water from the ceiling into a garbage pail. Workers said the pail, intended as a quick fix, had been in place for two weeks while they awaited repairs... .

---

65   "Eddie's Master Stroke," *Bloomberg Businessweek*, November 28, 2004, http://www.businessweek.com/stories/2004-11-28/eddies-master-stroke.

"Dozens of products — from contact lens solution to dolls — were sold out. The store did not have enough inventory or employees to replace them on the shelves. Much of the commodity merchandise that was in stock was more expensive than at nearby competitors."[66]

This pattern of underfunding potentially big ideas played out in several other big innovations known as mygofer.com and the Blue Crew. Mygofer was designed as a way to let people buy online at low prices and pick up goods that day in a nearby Kmart or have them delivered, but the site was hard to use, and inventory was eccentric. A visitor looking for bakery goods, for instance, found precisely one item listed: a banana nut muffin mix. Razor blades cost three times as much as in a local Safeway. The Blue Crew was more ambitious. It was a variant of an idea we proposed to Arthur Martinez when he was CEO of Sears in the late 1990s. Our idea would have had Sears riding the Internet into services and using its brand name to become the nation's handyman. But the Blue Crew didn't go very far in that direction. The Blue Crew seemed to mostly be a way to try to sell products. The initial page online was full of products and offered advice on how to pick the best one. It was hard to even find a button to click to request repair service. More recently, Lampert announced a series of technology pushes, including a loyalty program, but investing was so tepid that there was never a chance to move the needle.

Despite what even his detractors describe as financial genius, Lampert has found no ways to reverse the slide at the combination of Kmart and Sears. Sales have slipped steadily from a combined $60 billion in 2005 to less than $40 billion in 2012. Profits have turned into heavy losses. The company, whose illustrious roots go back to the late 1800s and which spent decades as the dominant US retailer, seems to have begun a slow liquidation.

---

66   Gretchen Morgenson, Michael Barbaro, and Geraldine Fabrikant, "Saving Sears Doesn't Look Easy Anymore," *New York Times*, January 27, 2008, http://www. nytimes.com/2008/01/27/business/27eddie.html?pagewanted=all.

The other problem with traditional finance methods is that they distort or even short-circuit the learning process. By definition, disruptive innovations deal with future scenarios that are hard to read and where the right strategy is not clear; the right strategy has to emerge over time. But, "we'll figure it out as we go" doesn't fit in with traditional finance and planning mindsets. By forcing detailed projections too early, the finance department can limit experimentation and adaptation.

Net present value provides a good example. It can be a great tool for looking at the return that an investment will provide. However, its use can carry two weaknesses.

One is that the most important factor in net present value is the profits that are expected well into the future. No one knows, especially with a big innovation project, what those profits will be, so they're subject to debate. How can you project customer interest for a product that customers haven't yet seen? When even a small change in assumptions can make an investment in innovation look like anything between a killer app and idiocy, there's a lot on the line. So the debate really becomes a proxy for corporate power. If a company's existing operations get to write the numbers, they may push for assumptions that will translate into a painfully low net present value for new ideas—lest new investment areas threaten existing operations. If those pushing for innovation have the upper hand, rosy assumptions might be used to justify what will be a killer flop.

"Very often when you are going for real innovation, you have to go against prevailing wisdom," said Dr. Robert Langer, who heads a Massachusetts Institute of Technology lab that has spun out dozens of successful medical companies and has been a consultant at large pharmaceutical companies. "And it's hard to go against prevailing wisdom when there are people who have been there for a long time and you have some vice president who says, 'No, that doesn't make sense.'"[67]

67 Hannah Seligson, "Hatching Ideas, and Companies, by the Dozen at MIT," *New York Times*, November 24, 2012, http://www.nytimes.com/2012/11/25/business/mit-lab-hatches-ideas-and-companies-by-the-dozens.html?pagewanted=1&ref=general&src=me.

The second weakness with net present value calculations stems from the fact that the uncertain nature of calculations is generally hidden. The way people are wired, we often treat numbers and models with more respect than they deserve.

At one large organization where we conducted an innovation stress test, people were uncomfortable with a financial forecast but weren't inclined to tackle it; it had more than 90 tabs, full of numbers out to two or three decimal places, so it had the feel of truth. In fact, in less than a minute, once we asked a few questions about the high-level assumptions that were baked into the model, the flaws became obvious to all. The model assumed that our client would get more than 50 percent share in a new market, right out of the gate, even though no company held even a 10 percent share, and our client had no reason to expect to be the leader initially. No one was being dishonest or even devious. No one tried to hide the assumptions. It's just that the management team treated the numbers with too much respect. Once they scaled back expectations, they saved a lot of money and gave themselves time to build a solid business. But many organizations just plow ahead, without challenging some highly dubious numbers.

So, while all the other rules that we offer are about what to do, this rule is more about what not to do, which is to *not* use traditional financial measures for evaluating big innovations. Sure, use these tried-and-true financial measures for the businesses that you understand well, because the measures are valid there. But don't pretend to have numerical certainty about new ideas before you really know what will happen.

Remember, something isn't much of an innovation if the results are instantly and totally transparent. Besides, someone else would have already come up with the idea.

Instead, take a more iterative approach to understanding the finances of new businesses. This will be hard. Many executives get antsy if you tell them they can't do their numerical analysis. So, a culture has to be established, beginning at the very top of the organization, which says that newborns get to crawl and walk and maybe even start preschool before their talents are evaluated.

IBM shows what can happen when you defer decisions until you have real data.

By the early 1990s, IBM had a long history of applying financial screens too early and, as a result, rejecting innovation—nothing seemed to measure up when compared with the 80 percent gross margins IBM generated on its mainframes and related software from the 1960s until well into the 1980s. So, IBM pretty much ignored minicomputers when Digital Equipment pioneered the market. IBM invented technology that became core to workstations but lost the market to Sun Microsystems and others. IBM's PC introduction in 1981 made that market explode, but IBM crushed its PC business (after ceding the extraordinarily profitable pieces to Intel and Microsoft). IBM could have owned all sorts of businesses related to its core computers—storage, printers, networking, and so on—but never moved fast enough.

Then, in the early 1990s, IBM made a small bet that tested a new possibility: Services could be an important business. There was certainly reason to think so. All the major accounting firms, led by Arthur Andersen, were building huge computer consulting businesses. Electronic Data Systems (EDS) served as an even more pointed indicator of the possibilities for IBM—its founder, H. Ross Perot, had been a top salesman at IBM and tried to get the company to expand into services, before striking out on his own in 1962 and making a fortune. Services didn't meet the exacting standards of IBM's financial reviews. The business would generate gross margins of only 10 percent to 15 percent. So, although outsourcing of corporate IT departments was becoming popular in the early 1990s, IBM didn't bid on contracts. Fortunately for IBM, its chief marketing executive at the time, George Conrades, had both the vision and the clout to try services anyway.

When a particularly big customer decided to outsource, Conrades worried that an EDS or Andersen Consulting would win the contract and set a troubling precedent. IBM still had CIOs convinced that it provided job security through superior equipment and overwhelming service—the line was, "Nobody ever got fired for buying IBM"—but competitors were making inroads, and IBM was feeling the heat. The CIO of a major brokerage on Wall Street said he had what he called his "million-dollar coffee mug." Anytime an IBM salesman quoted him a price on a mainframe, he'd pour himself a cup of coffee in a mug from Amdahl, a mainframe maker, and the salesman would knock $1 million off the quote.[68] If a services company won the big outsourcing contract, kicked IBM equipment out, and still kept running smoothly, CIOs at lots of big companies might develop the confidence to get rid of the IBM security blanket. Their bosses might demand that they do so rather than keep paying a hefty premium for IBM products.

Faced with both a threat and an opportunity, Conrades overrode internal concerns, bid on the outsourcing contract, and won. When early results were favorable, IBM bid on another big contract and won that, too. If the contracts hadn't worked out, IBM could have just moved on, none the worse for wear. But they did work, so some executives rallied around services, and IBM kept building the business.

The business was eventually going to have conflicts with existing divisions over resources, how to price IBM products, when to buy equipment from competitors, and so on, but the financial crisis that beset IBM and that lasted through the mid-1990s created such an existential scramble that any big financial tests were deferred. There

---

68   Paul B. Carroll. *Big Blues: The Unmaking of IBM*. New York: Crown Publishers, 1993.

were so many problems to solve that nobody was going to complain much about a business simply because it didn't meet IBM's historical standards of profitability. No business was meeting IBM's historical standards.

Louis Gerstner, who arrived as CEO in 1993, approached the business with the right "let's figure this out as we go along" approach. While the former McKinsey partner is a highly analytical type, his memoirs suggest that he analyzed only what would produce real numbers. For instance, he commissioned an analysis of IBM's efforts to sell software applications to corporate clients and found that IBM had invested about $20 billion in the apps, in exchange for only about $6 billion in total revenue. Gerstner killed the apps business despite loud protests. With services, however, if he had commissioned the typical financial review, he would have received guesses dressed up as numbers. While it would have been plausible to look at other services businesses such as EDS and see their revenue and profits, moving IBM into services was going to affect margins and revenue in every other part of IBM's business in complex ways that couldn't be determined ahead of time. Gerstner knew, in a nonquantitative way, that customers valued IT services and would pay. After all, he had been a huge consumer of IT services when he ran American Express's card operations and then became CEO of RJ Reynolds. He valued anyone who could reduce the complexity of running huge data centers, and he wanted IBM to play that role as widely as possible. So, he provided resources to the new services business, monitored its progress and its effects on other parts of the company, and made course corrections as he went along. The business thrived.

The last two CEOs—Samuel Palmisano, who succeeded Gerstner in 2002, and Ginni Rometty, who succeeded Palmisano in 2012—have come out of the services business, and IBM has made the tricky transition away from a total reliance on what used to be called "big iron," where margins have come under pressure as computing power becomes a commodity more like electricity. As of 2012, the company had returned $137 billion to shareholders in the form of dividends and share repurchases since 2000 and expects to return $70 billion more by 2015.[69] The stock trades at or near all-time highs.

As IBM shows, financial analysis can be great, but only when it's based on real numbers. Many attempts at innovation are analyzed too soon, when numbers are based on potentially dangerous biases.

Meanwhile, competitors that didn't Start Small, later panicked, bet big, and flopped. HP, for instance, bought EDS for $13.9 billion in 2008 in an attempt to build, overnight, the kind of capability IBM had been nurturing for almost two decades. In 2012—two CEOs later—HP wrote down the value of EDS by a whopping $8 billion.[70] Dell bought Perot Systems in 2009 for $3.9 billion. While Dell hasn't taken a write-down, it is flailing on all fronts.[71]

---

69   Shara Tibken, "IBM Increases Dividend 13%," *Wall Street Journal*, April 24, 2012, http://online.wsj.com/article/SB10001424052702303459004577363800998248924.html?mod=WSJ_hp_LEFTWhatsNewsCollection.

70   We're not just criticizing this deal in hindsight. Based on our research for *Billion Dollar Lessons*, we trashed the idea in this blog post in August 2008: http://www.devilsadvocategroup.com/infosys-and-hewlett-packard-consultants-heal-thyselves/.

71   We didn't like this deal, either. We wrote this blog post in September 2009: http://www.devilsadvocategroup.com/dell-pulls-the-trigger-and-shoots-itself-in-the-foot/.

~ *Rule 5*
Get Everyone on the Same Page

L et's assume you've done all the things we've recommended thus far. You understand your technology context. You've explored your doomsday scenarios and developed a good grasp of competitive challenges and strategic risks. You've started from a clean sheet of paper and understand how you might reinvent your company, putting it into idealized form. You've forestalled any attempts to kill an innovation prematurely. Now, emboldened with a clear sense of the answer, you want to get on with it.

That would be a mistake.

Leaders must mobilize their organizations before they can start implementing their visions. But leaders often skip the mobilization step and fail as a result. John Kotter, a Harvard Business School professor who is regarded as an expert on business transformations, said that in more than half of those he studied leaders failed to create enough urgency to spur action. Kotter said executives often tell him, "Oh, no, no, lack of urgency is not an issue—our people understand how important it is to solve this problem. We're beyond that."[72] But, he says, "Executives underestimate how hard it can be to drive people out of their comfort zones."

---

72 Interview with John Kotter, *Management Consulting News*, 2013, http://management consultingnews.com/interview-john-kotter/

No matter how good the CEO's vision, you can't be a leader if you don't have followers. So, after defining the vision, it's crucial to step back, assess where the organization is, and identify impediments to change.

The first decision you have to make concerns whether it's even possible to get everyone on the same page, because in some cases it isn't. If a carmaker decides, for instance, to deal directly with car owners, including diagnosing problems and upgrading the software in cars remotely, car dealers may simply refuse to go along. They make so much of their money from service that the manufacturers may simply be unable to compensate them enough for the change in control of the customer relationship. State laws typically protect the local dealers so thoroughly that dealers might well be able to stymie what the carmakers see as essential innovations. If an innovation would have to kill the core business to succeed, it also won't be possible to get everyone on the same page. Those in the existing business will always try to kill rather than be killed.

In some cases, you can delay an uprising by being discreet. For instance, insurance companies are publicly working with agents to try to justify their existence in a time when people can easily buy just about any type of insurance online less expensively, without an agent, but we assume the insurers are also experimenting quietly with ways of cutting out the agents.

In other cases, where those not on the same page can't cripple you—as car dealers could cripple manufacturers and as insurance agents could cripple the companies writing the insurance—you can be overt and simply pit a new business against the existing one. The caveat, of course, is that the new business has to be sheltered enough that it has a real chance and isn't simply crushed in its early days.

This sort of honest competition is what happened at Dayton-Hudson. The five Dayton brothers had taken over the family department-store business in the 1950s and expanded into the suburbs. In 1958, they heard about the concept of discounting and decided to test it, despite plenty of misgivings. One of the brothers explored discounting as a separate business and was allowed to compete as hard as he wanted against Dayton-Hudson. Another ran the traditional business. If we tell you that the new business was named Target, you'll know that the new business won. In fact, it eventually subsumed Dayton-Hudson. Of the more than 300 department-store chains in the United States in the late 1950s, only Dayton-Hudson/Target successfully moved into discount retailing.

If you decide that you can, in fact, get everyone on the same page, then you're ahead of the game. But you may still step into a huge trap. It's often clear that a culture needs to change: The organization needs to be faster, more innovative, more disciplined, more something else. So an executive, especially if she's new to the organization, describes a new culture and hands out marching orders.

Don't do it. Culture eats strategy for breakfast.

Culture is powerful and hard to change. Just issuing orders won't do. Even pulling the classic levers—measuring change, replacing those who balk, implementing a compensation system that reinforces the desired change—may not be enough.

Cultures aren't written down. (Actually, some are, but the words almost always reflect wishful thinking that has little to do with how people act.) Yet any major change has to fit within the cultural norms. Context is key. A new approach might take at Southwest Airlines but not at United. If business units and frontline personnel are accustomed to autonomy, they'll find ways to resist if decision rights are taken away from them.

In addition, culture is multifaceted; different parts of an organization may operate very differently. The folks in manufacturing likely don't resemble those in sales and marketing. Operations in California may look very different than operations in Kentucky. Your investors have a culture; they may actually resist innovation because they're looking for a steady, low-risk flow of dividends. Your customers have a culture, too. Knight-Ridder's advertisers resisted Tony Ridder's attempts to move them online, while the digitally comfortable advertisers at IDG's computer publications made the transition eagerly.

Many executives believe they can change a culture to suit a strategy, rather than try to make the strategy fit the culture—and plenty of change-management groups will assure executives that what they want is possible. But it's better to simply work with what you've got.

That doesn't mean that leaders can't adopt change programs. Such programs can work. Cultures can even be changed. It's just that our research into failures found that change could take much longer than companies expect. Cultural change is a long-term issue that can rarely be counted on to solve an imminent problem or help take advantage of a short-term opportunity. When aspiring strategies clash against cultures, culture wins.

To succeed, then, leaders who want to get everyone on the same page must come to grips with the complexity of their many corporate cultures. Then, leaders must spend the time to get everyone in sync— within the constraints of the existing culture.

Leaders must not only create a general sense of urgency, they have to create a personal one. A general sense of urgency is when people say that something needs to be done, but mostly by someone else. When there's a personal sense of urgency, people are willing to do something themselves—for instance, ceding resources to an important new project rather than assuming the resources will come from elsewhere or even explicitly telling the project's leaders to fend for themselves. Leaders often make the mistake of thinking a general sense of urgency is enough, because they assume everyone has something like their sense of anxiety about the health of the entire organization. But people can be very provincial. They need to believe that a change will help them individually.

Robert Nardelli's experience at Home Depot shows the perils of acting too quickly without coming to grips with a culture. Motorola shows what can happen when you get the cultural issues right.

Nardelli had been a golden boy at General Electric but lost out in the race to succeed Jack Welch as CEO in 2000. Within 10 minutes of the GE board's decision, Home Depot approached Nardelli, and within days he became CEO of Home Depot. The company had grown so fast that it hit $40 billion in revenue just two decades after the first store was opened in Atlanta in 1978. But by the time Nardelli arrived as CEO in December 2000, the wheels were coming off. Archrival Lowe's was hurting Home Depot with bright, modern stores that were drawing crowds of women, and Walmart was moving into Home Depot's market. In the year before Nardelli's arrival, Home Depot's stock had fallen almost 50 percent.

Nardelli was hailed as the solution. Home Depot's stock went up almost 18 percent, about $10 billion of market value, when Nardelli accepted the CEO post.

Nardelli quickly moved to centralize control and instill discipline. Shocked at technology systems so outdated he couldn't send an e-mail to all managers at the same time, he invested billions of dollars in new technology. He launched major initiatives to remodel stores. After market surveys showed that customers wanted more choices in the paint department, every Home Depot store was reset in 90 days with a new technologically advanced color center. He stressed the urgency for change. One executive said Nardelli would tell people, "'I'm not looking at the calendar; I'm looking at my watch.'"[73]

What Nardelli did not do was get everyone on the same page. He paid little attention to Home Depot's culture and simply assumed that he could impose his will as he had within the blunt culture at GE.

---

73   Claudia H. Deutsch, "A Do-It-Yourselfer Takes on Home Depot," *New York Times*, July 29, 2001, http://www.nytimes.com/2001/07/29/business/29NARD. html.

Home Depot's culture was extremely entrepreneurial and very customer-focused when Nardelli arrived.[74] Yet, Nardelli immediately eliminated the decision-making powers of whole layers of people. In an attempt to cut costs, he also undermined the culture of customer service by replacing thousands of full-time employees with part-time workers at Home Depot's stores. Those full-time employees, known as the "experts in the aisle," were the secret sauce at Home Depot, as just about any employee or customer could have told Nardelli. Nardelli further alienated the troops at Home Depot because, when he dismissed managers who didn't meet his performance targets, he often filled their posts with former executives from GE. That led some bitter insiders to dub the company "Home GEpot."

With Nardelli leading but few following, the anger among employees led to dissatisfaction among customers. In 2005, Home Depot scored the lowest among major US retailers in the University of Michigan's annual American Consumer Satisfaction index, 11 points lower than Lowe's and even three points lower than Kmart.

By most measures, Nardelli's quantitative results were quite good. Sales soared from $46 billion in 2000, the year Nardelli took over, to $81.5 billion in 2005, an average annual growth rate of 12 percent. Profits more than doubled, to $5.8 billion. Nardelli's relentless cost-cutting drove gross margins from 30 percent in 2000 to 33.8 percent in 2005.

But Nardelli never won over employees or customers, and never convinced analysts and investors of the strategic rationale behind the sterling numbers or of their sustainability. During Nardelli's tenure, Home Depot's stock value actually dropped 6 percent, while Lowe's jumped nearly 200 percent. The board asked Nardelli in late 2006 to revamp his lavish compensation agreement. After negotiations failed, Nardelli resigned.

---

74   According to a report by Barry Henderson, an equities analyst at T. Rowe Price.

His successor, Frank Blake, continued many of the efficiency-related changes that Nardelli had made but focused anew on customer service and took great care with the culture. Although Blake is also a product of the command-and-control culture at GE—he was the general counsel—he made it known that he was consulting regularly with founders Bernie Marcus and Arthur Blank, who remained totems for employees. Each weekend, he handwrote dozens of notes to employees, most often to thank them for providing great service to a customer. He exhibited a low-key persona, wandering around stores with a cup of Dunkin' Donuts coffee in his hand. Blake became known as the "calmer in chief" at Home Depot. Not coincidentally, as of this writing, its stock is up 86 percent since Nardelli left. Lowe's is up 27 percent.

In contrast with Nardelli, Sanjay Jha took his time and came to grips with the Motorola culture when he was brought in as co-CEO in 2008 and asked to turn around Motorola's cell phone business, with an eye toward spinning it off.

The company was in horrible shape. Its share of the US mobile phone market had dropped from 60 percent in the late 1990s to 7 percent in 2008. Jha, who had been COO of Qualcomm, had to slash costs to contend with rapidly eroding sales—which plunged even faster when the Great Recession hit, within months of his arrival. He estimated that if he didn't deliver successful products for Christmas 2009, less than 14 months after his arrival, Motorola was finished. Yet he had to turn Motorola around with an organization that had missed just about every major transition in the cell phone market: "1G to 2G, 2G to 3G, black-and-white to color, to camera, to touch, to QWERTY" keyboards, in Jha's words. "We, as an organization, missed a lot of transitions."[75]

---

75   Saul Hansell, "How Sanjay Jha Overhauled Motorola's Culture," *New York Times,* October 29, 2009, http://bits.blogs.nytimes.com/2009/10/29/how-sanjay-jha-overhauled-motorolas-culture/

That organization was focused on fighting the last war—mostly with itself—instead of contending with the new demands of the marketplace. "On my thirteenth day on the job, I had a meeting with Vodafone," the world's largest wireless carrier, Jha said. Three separate Motorola product groups pitched their handset ideas. "The Vodafone executive said, 'Wow. Could you please pick one device and let me know what you think I should buy?'"

Jha found numerous, autonomous efforts devoted to the next generation of the RAZR voice-oriented phone and little effort to make the transition to smartphones. In fact, there were few concerted efforts of any sort. While competitors like Nokia built phones around a few standard designs and components, Motorola used a jumble of chips, phone parts, and operating systems. Jha found twenty-two different phone displays, each requiring different software.

Jha could have come in and started issuing orders, as Nardelli had at Home Depot. After all, Jha knew what needed to be fixed. Instead, even though the problems were far more urgent at Motorola than at Home Depot, Jha took the time to build support. He likely had an advantage because Motorola has an engineering culture, where arguments can carry the day as long as people get a chance to air their views and aren't simply ordered to change their thinking. And Jha understood the culture. He has a PhD in electronic and electrical engineering, began his career as a design engineer, and came from an organization, Qualcomm, whose engineering focus is similar to Motorola's.

To get everyone on the same page, and to build the relationships and trust he needed to drive Motorola's transformation, Jha drilled into the details. He met with the top fifteen executives almost as soon as he arrived and asked them what was wrong with the company. He also met with employees and personally reviewed key projects throughout the company.

To build urgency, Jha held town hall meetings with groups of employees, and one of those meetings uncovered an effort that led to Motorola's salvation. In Silicon Valley, far from Motorola's Chicago-area headquarters, Jha met Rick Osterloh, who was working on a smartphone based on Google's Android operating system. Android was just one of many operating systems competing for attention in those days, but Osterloh impressed Jha. Within days, Jha returned to California and convened a meeting of the top dozen members of Osterloh's group. Making a point about urgency, Jha convened the four-hour meeting at 6:00 p.m. Jha asked for the team's hundred-slide presentation in advance and asked so many detailed questions that the team had to produce twenty more. Jha came away impressed.

Jha still gave the other groups their chance in coming weeks, but they didn't hold up to his scrutiny. Jha killed phones using several operating systems and settled on Android and a Microsoft mobile Windows operating system, but then Microsoft said a key release was being delayed. Jha settled on Android.

In his efforts to simplify development, Jha also had to pick microprocessors and radio chips that would be his standard parts. Among other choices, he had to decide whether to use a line of chips made by a division he used to run at Qualcomm or whether to use a design that Motorola had been developing with Texas Instruments. Unlike Nardelli, whose default position was to turn to his former employer, Jha chose the Motorola design.

In the fall of 2008, still quite early in Jha's time at Motorola, Verizon asked for a "long ball play" for the fourth quarter of 2009—meaning something that might be able to stand up to the onslaught of the iPhone. Jha made the bold decision to place a big bet, and the organization went along with him. "Sanjay said, 'Burn the ships and focus on Android,'" said Iqbal Arshad, who was put in charge of the Android project.

The rebound had begun. Motorola's new phone, which T-Mobile called Cliq and which Verizon called the Droid, was an instant hit. The Droid alone surpassed one million units by 50,000 in its first 74 days on the market. That may seem like an odd metric, but 74 days had become an industry benchmark because that's how long it took for the iPhone to sell its first million units.

Jha then reached beyond the formal hierarchy, identifying as many as 300 people whom he referred to as Motorola's "innovation class" and personally making sure they had the resources they needed to get their ideas to the next level.

Jha's approach to fixing Motorola was just right. Despite the need for a quick fix, he took the time to get the company on the same page. He fit his strategy within the culture, rather than try to change the culture. He made many changes—such as the innovation class—that would change the culture in the long term, but he didn't count on having those changes take effect in time to save the company.

Google announced in 2011 that it was buying the Motorola cell phone business for $12.5 billion, meaning the market cap for the company as a whole had more than doubled since Jha walked in the door in 2008.

To come to grips with your culture and understand how to get everyone on the same page for a potentially awkward transition to a new business model, you need to look for the kinds of problems that typically get glossed over when a CEO assumes that everyone feels his sense of urgency, that he can just issue orders, or that he can remold a culture quickly.

The best mechanism we know is one we have used often, to powerful effect. We call it a "future history." Have the executive team imagine that they're five years in the future, and ask them to write two memos of perhaps 750 to 1,000 words each.

For the first memo, have them imagine that a strategy has failed because of resistance from some parts of the organization, investors, or customers. The memo should explain the failure. The exercise lets people raise issues without being seen as naysayers, and seeing the rationale for failure in a clearly worded memo tends to crystallize thinking.

To heighten the effect, they can even do some formatting and write the memo so it looks like an article from the *Wall Street Journal* or *New York Times*. Everybody hates the idea of being embarrassed in such publications, so they pay attention to the potential problems and can address them while there's still time.

The second memo is the success story. What were the key elements and events that helped the organization shake its complacency? What were the key strategic shifts that helped to capture disruptive opportunities? How did the organization's unity help to beat the competition from existing players and start-ups? This part of the exercise encourages competitive war-gaming and helps the executive team understand the milestones on the critical path to success.

A note of caution: The tendency is to water down the failure memo/story and inflate the success memo/story to glorious heights. Resist that tendency. These memos are designed to highlight potential problems and roads to success, not to serve as predictions. If you and your team can agree ahead of time that you'll have a neutral observer chronicle the potential reasons for failure and for success, and then simply write them in story form, you gain an awful lot of insight.

The CEO of a major financial services company occasionally still reads to internal audiences parts of the future histories we wrote for him in early 2011 and says they helped him get his team focused on the right opportunities. As of this writing, his company's stock is up almost 60 percent since we wrote the memos, even though his competitors have had problems.

~ *Rule 6*
Build a Basket of Killer Options

You've come up with a great idea and protected it from premature financial analysis. You've taken the extra time to get everyone on board. You're finally ready to start investing in your killer app, right?

Yes, you're ready—but only to invest a bit.

You can't yet zero in on one idea, and you should invest as little as possible. At this stage in the innovation process, any given killer app idea is still more likely to fizzle than sizzle, so don't fall in love with a single idea just yet. We've seen a lot of companies waste an awful lot of money by plunging ahead with what they're sure is The Answer. What you've really developed thus far is a finely nuanced understanding of The Question. You can now go about testing possible killer apps, but those tests should be like a series of Petri dishes in a science lab.

"Nothing here. Nothing here. Nothing here. . . . Ah, here we seem to be growing something that's killing bacteria. Let's call it penicillin and go save millions of lives."

We refer to these tests as taking options, rather than as Petri dishes, largely because there's more familiarity with options in the world of business. People know that if you're worried about a possible surge in corn prices, you don't have to take delivery of a million bushels and store them somewhere. Instead, for a fraction of the price, you can purchase an option to buy the million bushels in the future at a guaranteed price. You might lose your modest investment, but you're protected if corn prices surge. People also generally know that stock options are issued to employees at a certain strike price and only "come into the money" if the stock moves north of the price at which the shares can be exercised.

The discipline around options in financial markets can be translated roughly into the world of what are sometimes called real options.[76] The main difference is that, while companies outside the financial services sector tend to use options to hedge against possible increases in commodity prices, options can be used for offense, not just defense. You can take an option on a killer app, pay a tiny fraction of the potential value, and still set yourself up to reap all the rewards.

If you have an idea that could turn into a multibillion-dollar business, you don't need to invest billions right away. You can invest millions of dollars, or even tens of thousands, to start testing your killer app in a structured way that preserves the option for that multibillion-dollar business but doesn't require much up-front investment and gives you plenty of outs along the way.

Structuring investments as options, rather than full-fledged, go-to-market plans, also helps you afford to test more ideas. In addition, little tests can be cycled through faster than full-scale implementations, and cycle time is crucial when it comes to innovating. If you give us two moves in a chess match for every one you take, we'll beat you every time, no matter who you are.

---

76   If we sound a bit gun-shy, it's because financial engineers fell in love with the math for options, convinced themselves that they could make massive bets without risk, and plunged the world's financial system into chaos. Long-Term Capital Management, a hedge fund that was founded on the idea of riskless bets and that employed the two men who won the Nobel Prize in Economics for developing the widely used Black-Scholes model, failed in the late 1990s and threatened the stability of the world's financial system. AIG, which used similar math to justify extraordinary exposure to subprime mortgages, collapsed in 2008 and helped usher in the most painful recession since the Depression. The use of options in financial markets has lessons to offer, but they have to be kept in perspective. No investment is without risk, no matter how fancy the math and no matter how many Nobel Prize winners stand behind the idea.

A classic example of a real option that was handled well was Lotus Notes. In 1984, a talented programmer named Raymond Ozzie wanted to develop a product that would help PC users work together in groups. Lotus founder Mitchell Kapor liked the idea but recognized the many uncertainties. Ozzie's idea didn't just depend on the usual difficulties associated with a complex software-development project or with pioneering a market that had drawn zero interest from users—difficulties that are plenty daunting. Ozzie's idea also required that e-mail be widely adopted, that local area networks become ubiquitous, and that Microsoft's then-awful operating system, Windows, have robust multitasking capabilities. All those assumptions were highly uncertain in 1984. So, Lotus set up Ozzie's project, known as Notes, as an option. Lotus agreed to finance Notes but reviewed the project at regular intervals and had the contractual right to stop financing at anytime. If Lotus kept providing funds, it had the exclusive right to bring Notes to market. If Lotus stopped, though, then Ozzie could take the project elsewhere, even to a competitor like Microsoft. The approach let Lotus limit its exposure to Notes, only stepping up investment once technical and market hurdles were cleared. The approach also kept Lotus honest at each review, encouraging it to assess fairly the likely value of Notes, even though many in the spreadsheet business, Lotus's breadwinner, wanted to cut funding or even kill the project.

It took five years to develop Notes and determine that there really was a market. The product started slowly when it was introduced in 1990 but then developed a following and soon became the core of Lotus's business. When IBM bought Lotus for $3.5 billion in a hostile takeover in 1995, it was Notes, not the 1-2-3 spreadsheet, that IBM coveted.

By contrast, we witnessed the aftermath at a large financial services company that plunged ahead with a business rather than structure it as a real option. (We were brought in to stress test the idea after the initial failure, to see if it had a future. It didn't. We have since steered the company toward the use of options.) The company had done a reasonable job of following our first five rules. It understood its technology context. The company focused on a true doomsday scenario; in fact, the killer app idea was in direct response. The company mostly started with a clean sheet of paper in envisioning a future. Finally, the company avoided premature financial analysis and had everyone on the same page, though with a caveat. Plenty of people on the executive team doubted the idea but were willing to give it the benefit of the doubt both because the idea came from the CEO and because the CEO had founded the business on a similar hunch and had built a multibillion-dollar market cap. The idea was a true killer app, too. It would have changed our client's business and set it up well for at least a decade. When it came time to start testing the idea, though, the company lost patience, simply assumed the idea would work, and invested heavily. Minimal testing would have shown that the idea both was not technically feasible and not even remotely interesting to the market. Instead, the company wasted tens of millions of dollars on the project. The company also distracted itself for some two years rather than getting started on the real work that must be done to deal with that doomsday scenario that is still out there waiting.

In setting up a portfolio, the obvious question is: What are my possible killer apps? But that requires a long answer, and it helps to know how many to shoot for, so we'll start with the narrower, technical question: How many killer options should you be investigating at any given time?

The answer depends partly on how many breakthrough ideas you can come up with, but we can be a bit more specific than that. You certainly need to have more than one, and you probably should have no more than five.

The more-than-one contention is easy to prove: Technological change can be so confusing and uncertain that it just doesn't make sense to have only one alternative—as our financial services client learned the hard way.

Navistar took a diversified approach to innovation for years and continually brought out important new products,[77] but then the CEO made a $700 million bet on a single, crucial technology. The plan was to drastically reduce emissions to meet new standards from the Environmental Protection Agency and, in the process, revolutionize truck engines—but the technology didn't work. Navistar fell well behind competitors, which met the standards in a conventional way. Navistar is teetering because of thousands of dollars of fines that it has to pay for each nonconforming engine it sells.[78] The idea for the new technology wasn't necessarily a bad one, and companies sometimes get away with taking a single roll of the dice. But meeting the new standards was too important for the CEO to bet on just one approach, especially an unconventional one. Instead, the CEO should have figured out how to structure small tests of the new technology while spending enough on the approach used by the rest of the industry that he could have brought it to market if his more radical plan failed. With investors calling for his head, the CEO resigned in August 2012.[79]

Big pharmaceutical companies used to be very careful about assembling portfolios of possibilities for new drugs, but, with patents expiring for drugs that generate hundreds of billions of dollars a year in revenue, panicky managers are increasingly placing huge bets on what those in the industry call "product shots"—individual possibilities that

---

77   Joe Cahill, "Suits Can Innovate, Too," *Crain's Chicago Business,* April 2, 2012, http://www.chicagobusiness.com/article/20120331/ISSUE01/303319959/suits-can-innovate-too.

78   Todd J. Behme, "Navistar Opts to Retreat from Engine Technology," *Crain's Chicago Business,* July 3, 2012, www.chicagobusiness.com/article/20120703/NEWS05/120709964/navistar-opts-to-retreat-from-engine-technology-report.

79   Alejandra Cancino, "Amid Troubles, Navistar CEO Dan Ustian Retires," *Chicago Tribune,* August 28, 2012, http://articles.chicagotribune.com/2012-08-28/business/ct-biz-0828-navistar-ceo--20120828_1_dan-ustian-stephen-volkmann-navistar-international-corp.

could single-handedly replace a drug like Lipitor, which went off patent in 2011.[80] The product shots have almost all failed, and pharmaceutical companies have seen their drug pipelines drying up. The companies have had to resort to buying small companies to find innovative drugs.

Knowing the upper limit for killer options is a bit trickier. Many people argue that a corporate innovation portfolio should be like a venture capital portfolio, which may include dozens of investments. Consultants and authors argue that companies should back "intrapreneurs" and adopt the financial tools that VCs use to evaluate investments and so on, to simulate VC successes as closely as possible. The analogy makes some sense because many VC funds have delivered spectacular returns for decades and have been much more innovative than most corporations. VCs keep the market for G5s healthy; why not just do what they do?

While we began our collaboration in the 1990s assuming that VCs had a lot to teach businesses, we soon learned that large businesses are not VC funds—and are almost certainly doomed to fail if they try to be. History shows that acting like a real VC fund and having dozens of killer options doesn't work. IBM set up a sort of VC fund in the 1980s to invest in PC software companies, and Intel invested in a portfolio of companies in the late 1990s that might help it into related technologies, but both efforts failed even though the market dominance of IBM and Intel meant they could offer an awful lot more help than a VC ever could. Some companies, including Kodak and General Motors, set up venture organizations in Silicon Valley, hoping the fairy dust would rub off. They failed. We're not aware of a single major company that set up a venture fund and succeeded in our terms: coming up with an innovation so fundamental that it ushered in the next phase of a business.

---

80   David Shaywitz, "Is Big Pharma Dangerously Betting on Huge, Fragile Product Shots?" *Forbes*, November 5, 2012, http://www.forbes.com/sites/davidshaywitz/2012/11/05/is-big-pharma-dangerously-betting-on-huge-fragile-product-shots/.

Much of the reason that a portfolio doesn't work relates to senior-management attention. There's only so much of it available in a big company. No CEO can keep track of one or two dozen nascent businesses while still running a multibillion-dollar company day to day. The CEO can't delegate the work, either. No option that might fundamentally change, say, Blockbuster from physical rentals done in stores to a mail-order or streaming business can survive without a CEO's nurturing. If killer options exist simply as a broad portfolio, without CEO backing, it's impossible to meet the other two requirements of starting small: neutralizing traditional financial analysis until the appropriate time and getting everyone on the same page. Everyone would be free to do what they've always done. The status quo would always win.

Motorola, for instance, had a great record of producing innovative ideas even in the days leading up to its near-death experience. But those ideas would get to the $2 million level in annual revenue, then be folded into a business unit with revenue targets of $1 billion or more, according to a colleague who was a senior executive at Motorola. The innovations would get lost and ultimately die.

Besides, some decisions have to be made at the CEO level. At GM, for instance, in the late 1990s, the OnStar telematics system had shown real promise, but many in the traditional business argued that it should be offered only as an option on GM cars or, perhaps, used only to enhance the appeal of pricey Cadillacs. The limited approach would have doomed OnStar. The adoption would have been too slow. OnStar would have taken too long to get to the critical mass needed to support its centralized services. But installing OnStar as standard equipment meant an enormous financial risk—initially more than $1,000 per car, and GM makes a lot of cars. What if nobody paid the annual fee to subscribe? GM's CEO at the time, Rick Wagoner, made the call that the warring factions beneath him couldn't make and installed OnStar across most of the product line. He made the right call. Despite all the nastiness that has hit GM over the past decade-plus, OnStar has been a good business for GM and has let it learn all kinds of things about what buyers do with its cars and about the cars themselves. GM, for example, can gather operational data from millions of cars on the road through OnStar, whereas it previously had to rely on computer simulations and a small number of test cars. Estimates indicate that hundreds of millions of dollars in warranty costs have been averted each year. Analysts now estimate that OnStar generates $1.5 billion in annual revenue and, as a stand-alone business, would be valued at $5 billion to $7 billion.[81]

The limits on senior management's attention are actually just the beginning of the problems with setting up a huge portfolio of options. Here are the others:

- **Portfolios set the wrong priorities.** A CEO needs to test ideas that might lead to a bright, new future, but a portfolio manager merely wants the best possible return on investment. The priorities don't mesh.

  Portfolio managers often invest far outside a core business to avoid any internal entanglements. Managers certainly aren't going to back anything that the main existing business might see as a threat and kill. That's part of the reason that Florida Progress Corp., a utility, tried in the early 1990s to invest in a Major League Baseball franchise rather than look for some breakthrough in its core business.

  Even if a portfolio manager, well, hits a home run, it almost surely won't matter to the company as a whole. If someone takes $20 million and earns a 50 percent annual return for several years, that won't move the needle for a multibillion-dollar company.

81   Deepa Seetharaman, "GM's Connected Car: Brought to You By Allstate?" *Automotive News*, May 4, 2013, http://www.autonews.com/article/20130504/OEM06/130509931/gms-connected-car:-brought-to-you-by-allstate?goback=%2Egde_4731574_member_241911849#axzz2TZeE5Hu6.

- **Failure at a start-up differs from failure at a big company.** Entrepreneurs who fail can take some street cred when they move on to the next venture. They've been there, done that. Backers often see them as more qualified for the next run. At big companies, by contrast, failure typically derails careers.

  So, failures at corporate ventures need to be managed carefully, and that's perilously difficult with a portfolio. The CEO needs to be involved enough to know when an idea failed because of bad execution versus when it failed simply because the future turned out to be different than it might have been. David Pottruck, former CEO of Charles Schwab, talks about "noble failures." These are the ideas that were tested well but that simply didn't pan out. Pottruck says businesses must recognize and celebrate their noble failures, including by publicly praising and perhaps even promoting those who ran them.

  Without creating the right culture of failure, businesses will find people reluctant to attempt new things. In addition, after launching a venture, companies will find it hard to kill even the worst ones, because anyone involved will do anything to avoid acknowledging being at a dead end.

- **Portfolio managers don't have all the answers.** While we, along with many others, sang the praises of VCs in the 1990s, the successes have drawn so many new people into the market that competition for great ideas is much tougher—in other words, VCs now operate in an environment that resembles the rest of the corporate world rather than having so much virgin territory to themselves. They're still plenty smart, but they're not magic, and they don't need to be imitated slavishly.

If dozens of killer options are too many, then what's the right number? In our experience, it's usually two to five. The result is what we call a basket of killer options, as opposed to the broad portfolios that VCs favor.

Figuring out what those killer options should be stems directly from the doomsday scenario and the clean sheet of paper we described in the Think Big section. Those exercises will prompt your thinking on what few options you need to invest in exploring to be sure that you're not rendered obsolete and that you see where you might leapfrog your competitors and seize the leadership of your industry.

Keep the following four principles in mind as you identify which killer options to test:

- **Those killer options really need to be killers.** Don't make the mistake of thinking that investing in the possibility of a better widget, even a much better widget, generates a killer option. Leave the incremental improvements to the incremental improvers. A killer option is the kind of test that took Apple from Macs to iPods to iPhones and to iPads. A killer option generates the possibility of a business that will either transform a company or generate a new business that kills the old one.

- **Play some poker.** Poker actually has a lot to say to executives, but, here, we're referring to the concept of pot odds. The notion is that you don't just figure out whether you have a better than even chance of winning a pot. You calculate what it will cost you, now and possibly after future cards, to compete for a pot. You compare that number with the size of the pot, then compare that ratio to what you think your odds of winning are. If you have to bet $1,000 to have a shot at a $10,000 pot, you could have just a one-in-five chance of winning and still be compelled to make that bet. We've said that the finance folks can't be very involved at this point, because all numbers are guesses, but you can still think in general terms about both the size of the investment and the size of the potential market.

- **Budget real time and real money.** If you don't set aside money specifically to investigate killer apps, you'll never do anything. When you come up with an idea for a killer option, you'll have to draw money away from existing businesses, giving them another reason to fight you. Similarly, you have to spec out regular time on your calendar to check on the progress of your killer options and, likely, to nurture them. Otherwise, the crush of business will overwhelm your best intentions.

- **Guard against the corporate antibodies, but be prepared to kill things yourself.** Just about every bias in an organization goes toward keeping the status quo. People are going to find every possible way to make a radically new idea fail. They'll try to steal the money or steal the people. They'll throw up technological obstacles. They may even get big customers to try to talk you out of the change. So, perhaps your most important job

is to block the antibodies long enough that your killer
options get every means to prove themselves before
you give up on them. If you have a manageable number
of options, you can probably protect them.

Here's one way to think about antibodies: Imagine that you're a
parent with two highly competitive boys, and you have to find ways to
keep them from crushing each other. That may seem flip, but we keep
coming across examples of companies where existing and new businesses were, in fact, run by brothers and had just the right relationship.
There was certainly competition in the air, but the parents made sure
the stronger brother couldn't put the weaker one in a headlock and give
him an endless noogie.

We've already mentioned Dayton-Hudson, where one brother
ran the traditional family business while another started up a discount
retailer, Target, which eventually overwhelmed Dayton-Hudson and a
whole lot of other retailers, besides. A similar situation played out at
IBM in the 1950s. Tom Watson Sr. had anointed Tom Jr. to be the next
CEO but also wanted to take care of his younger son, Dick. The solution
was to put Dick in charge of international operations and wall them off
from the rest of the business so that, even as CEO, Tom Jr. wouldn't
be able to boss his brother around much. Dick, wanting to show his
mettle, turned IBM's international operations into a blazing success,
far beyond what other information-products companies managed at
the time.

More recently, sibling rivalry worked at Pilot Flying J, a mostly
family-owned company that has more than 550 travel plazas in North
America, making it the largest such business. Jim Haslam founded
the business with a single gas station in Virginia in 1958 and built a
network of gas stations and convenience stores. As he brought his sons
into the business, he told them, "Jimmy, you take care of today, and Bill,
you take care of tomorrow." The basic business stayed healthy, while

the company developed a "travel center" concept that involved truck stops with branded fast food and expanded rapidly. The brothers did so well that Bill is now the governor of Tennessee, while Jimmy recently bought the Cleveland Browns.[82]

While it's important to head off the antibodies, you can't let bad ideas run forever. In the same way that those on the outside will feel threatened, those on the inside, possibly including the CEO, may fall in love with an idea.

Striking the right balance is hard (but, if it were easy, anybody could do it). Set up regular reviews, agreed to ahead of time, and decide at least once a year whether to continue funding. The analysis has to be done fresh each time, so you don't get carried away by the amount of money already invested. The question has to be: How much additional money will we need to invest, and might the bet be worthwhile? When a bet no longer looks good, set it aside, no matter how much financial and emotional capital has been poured in.

Netflix shows how ruthlessness can pay off. While it's mostly seen as the start-up that blew up Blockbuster, CEO Reed Hastings had planned from Day One to blow up his own business. He often notes that he didn't call his business DVDs by Mail; he named the business based on his belief that people would eventually stream their movies over the Internet. Even when his company was small, in the early 2000s, he invested heavily in technology that might let him stream video to consumers. But he repeatedly killed ventures when he saw they wouldn't quite work. He even had one technology ready to bring to market, one that would let consumers download a movie overnight. Then he saw YouTube and realized people would no longer wait for a download; transmission had to be instantaneous. So he killed that plan, too, despite everything he'd invested in it.

---

82   Associated Press, "Steelers Fan in Talks to Buy Browns," July 27, 2012, http://espn.go.com/nfl/story/_/id/8205396/pittsburgh-steelers-fan-jimmy-haslam-negotiations-purchase-cleveland-browns. In 2013, the FBI alleged a widespread scheme by Pilot Flying J to withhold rebates due to trucking customers, but as of this writing, nothing in the charges undercuts the basic success story at Pilot Flying J.

It's true that, when he finally built a huge streaming business, he tried to force the transition too quickly away from DVDs and raised prices in ways that sparked a backlash. Netflix lost customers, and investors clobbered the market valuation. Still, the willingness to kill so many bad ideas meant that Hastings managed innovation flawlessly for more than a decade and remained in the dominant position in terms of streaming.

He continued with his experimental approach, trying his hand at original programming with a cast of unknowns in a series filmed on location in Norway. (Talk about starting small.) The series, *Lilyhammer,* was a huge hit in Norway in early 2012, being viewed by one-fifth of the population. Hastings then brought the series to the United States, where it did well enough that he commissioned a higher-budget production, *House of Cards,* with big-name actors including Kevin Spacey and Robin Wright. That series became a sensation, partly because Netflix released all thirteen episodes at once and made *House of Cards* the best example yet of so-called binge viewing. The series drew lots of new subscribers, who typically stayed—and suddenly Netflix was looking hot again. Netflix followed with a comedy series, then another drama, *Hemlock Grove,* which critics panned but which drew even more viewers than *House of Cards.* Netflix released a new season of *Arrested Development,* which had been on Fox for three years, ending in 2006. Netflix is now exploring more original programming, including children's series.

By now, Netflix stock has mostly recovered from the thrashing it took after the overly hasty decision to move away from DVDs—perhaps the one time Hastings has given in to the temptation to start big. Having fallen from roughly $300 to $72, the stock, as of this writing, is back above $200. That gives Netflix a healthy valuation north of $12 billion. At busy parts of the day, a third of all Internet traffic is Netflix movies.

McDonald's took an even more deliberate approach to setting up options and shows the payoffs, while also demonstrating why a basket works better than a big portfolio.

After growing like crazy for decades through geographical expansion both in the United States and in just about every corner of the rest of the world, McDonald's had stagnated by the 1990s. Management tried to snap out of it by investing in a portfolio of options. McDonald's gave a rising star, a Swede named Mats Lederhausen, the job of assembling that portfolio. He and others at McDonald's did an unusually good job of buying all or parts of promising companies. For instance, McDonald's bought the vast majority of Chipotle for $350 million, expanded it nationally, and earned perhaps $1.2 billion when it cashed out. McDonald's took about a $300 million write-off on a pizza chain and had a mixed bag with its other investments: Pret a Manger, Boston Market, and a gourmet coffee chain. But that gain on Chipotle covers a lot of sins. McDonald's even invented Redbox. The initial idea was that people coming to McDonald's might also want grocery items such as eggs and milk, and an automated kiosk would let them buy those items inside McDonald's restaurants. Over time, McDonald's learned that what people really wanted were DVDs, and they didn't just want them at McDonald's. McDonald's eventually sold the business for about a $200 million gain. In all, McDonald's investments produced more than $1 billion of profit—nice work if you can get it.

As successful as those businesses were as investments, they had limited strategic value. They would have protected McDonald's if the world lost its hunger for burgers and fries and made a wholesale switch to, say, Mexican food but otherwise did nothing to help the main business innovate. Eventually, the investments failed the CEO-attention test and were all sold as too complicated to manage.

The best thing those investments accomplished was to show McDonald's the value of experimenting in innovation. In the 2000s, McDonald's turned that lesson on its core business and built a basket of killer options.

In some ways, McDonald's was the ideal setup for testing, because it had so many thousands of restaurants that could serve as labs. The initial idea for national ads came about when a franchisee in Minneapolis had sales go through the roof after he placed radio ads in the 1960s. Ronald McDonald came when a franchisee in Washington, DC, created a mini-circus as a promotion, and McDonald's headquarters took over the idea. The Big Mac came from a franchisee in Pittsburgh. The Filet-O-Fish and Egg McMuffin also came from franchisee experiments.

But McDonald's had strayed from its culture of testing and was left with a tired menu and tired facilities. Having seen through the investments in Chipotle and others that exploring new avenues could be profitable, McDonald's began to pursue options that might transform its core business.

The biggest risk was a move into coffee. McDonald's coffee was mostly known for a 1990s lawsuit in which a woman spilled coffee in her lap, sued the company, and won $640,000. It wasn't at all clear that McDonald's would have credibility if it tried to sell gourmet coffees and, even tougher, lattes and other high-end drinks. Those were Starbucks territory. But McDonald's tested and tested and tested and eventually got both the concept and all the operational details right.

McDonald's also began to take an experimental approach to its menu, trying out healthy items, including salads. The company tested free Wi-Fi. It tried new looks for its restaurants, making them much less like traditional fast-food places and more like family restaurants.

Not everything worked, of course. McDonald's tried a concept called Hearth Express that produced finer meals for people to take home. It turned out that patrons mostly wanted to eat in, and McDonald's didn't want to operate full-service restaurants, so the company killed the idea. But McDonald's had only built one restaurant, so the loss on the idea was teeny.

Some of the changes that McDonald's made border on the incremental, but, in total, they amounted to an attempt at transformation. McDonald's was reinventing itself as a healthy, modern alternative for the whole family and really stand out from the competition. Given that the competition's menus and facilities also felt tired when McDonald's began its transformation and didn't have McDonald's financial resources, McDonald's was hoping that they would be unable to duplicate McDonald's changes.

The approach worked. The company's share of the US burger market rose from 46 percent in 2006 to almost 50 percent in 2011.[83] The steady increase in revenue and profit fueled a more than sixfold surge in the stock price since the early 2000s. In other words, once McDonald's focused its innovation efforts on its core business and took a more focused approach to its options, it won big.

---

83   Joe Weisenthal, "Chart: US Burger Market Share (2006 vs. 2011), *Business Insider,* July 1, 2012, http://www.businessinsider.com/chart-us-burger-market-shares-2006-vs-2011-2012-7.

~ *Case Study*
Auto Insurance in a World Without Accidents

When Larry Page became CEO of Google in 2011, one of the first things he did was to implement an important concept of Start Small: He went through the vast portfolio of potential killer apps that had developed at Google and weeded out dozens. While the company doesn't specify the number of projects it's working on as part of Google X, it's now a modest, manageable total.

Google had already established a culture that kept the finance guys from weighing in on innovation too soon. Among other things, Google has told employees to set aside 10 percent of their time for self-defined projects and 20 percent for work on teams that aren't part of their core job—the kind of thing that makes a CFO freak but that Google's CFO has simply had to accept. Page and his predecessor, Eric Schmidt, have also mandated killer-option money for Google Labs, which is working on the driverless car, Google Glass, and other possible breakthroughs. Google has deliberately shortened planning horizons, which places a lower value on formal planning and gets close to the "let's figure it out as we go along" approach that more naturally fits innovation. When the head of Google's Android group was asked about his two-year plan, for instance, he said he didn't have one. He had a one-year plan that he tweaked every couple of months.[84]

---

84   Quentin Hardy, "Google's Innovation—and Everyone's?" *Forbes*, July 16, 2011, http://www.forbes.com/sites/quentinhardy/2011/07/16/googles-innova-

To get everyone on the same page, Google relies partly on its culture, but it also uses conventional approaches. For instance, when Google wanted to move into social media, Page announced that all bonuses would be tied to the success of Google+.

Now, we realize it's easier to set aside normal financial considerations when you're earning nearly $10 billion a year and have a net profit margin of 25 percent, as Google does—Google's profit works out to about $75,000 *per employee per quarter.* We also realize it's easier to keep everyone on the same page when you're a charismatic founder who shows up on every list of the world's richest people and who has helped make so many of the people around him rich, too.

So, we'll look at auto insurers to see how companies with a more normal set of advantages should Start Small in the face of a potentially major disruption like the Google driverless car.

At first blush, it would seem that car insurers should welcome the innovations coming out of research into driverless cars. Sensors will help keep drowsy or drunk drivers in their lanes and will slow or even stop a car when it might be about to hit something. Cameras embedded in cars could automatically film and then alert police to drunk or overly aggressive drivers, so they could either be pulled off the road immediately or at least visited the next day and warned. Drunk-driving deaths account for about one-third of US highway fatalities, and habitual DWI offenders are eight times as likely as those without DWI convictions to cause a drunk-driving fatality,[85] so there could be lots of opportunities to stop dangerous drivers before they cause an accident. (Again, this

---

tion-and-everyones/. Schmidt, who says he systematized innovation at Google, argues that companies in almost every industry can take an iterative approach that makes fast, incremental changes and feels its way to the future. Even if you're making a hammer, he says, you can do an instant 3-D print, send it out, learn what customers don't like, print an improvement, get more feedback and so on—and pretty soon you have the right hammer. He does rule out industries such as aviation, pharmaceuticals, and textbooks from this sort of approach because the regulatory approval process wouldn't allow constant iteration.

85   Traffic Safety Facts, 2009 Data, US Department of Transportation, National Highway Traffic Safety Administration, http://www-nrd.nhtsa.dot.gov/Pubs/811385.PDF.

prevention would have to occur within the limits of our tolerance for Big Brother—in this case, though, there wouldn't be many people who would stand up for the right to drive drunk.) Sensors built into cars should also reduce theft by making it possible to know where cars are at all times. (Already, in New York City, the number of cars stolen has declined from 147,000 in 1990 to 7,000 in 2011.)[86] From the standpoint of insurers, all these developments mean lower claims.

From a business standpoint, however, driverless cars might enable a long-term doomsday scenario for the roughly $200 billion in personal and commercial auto insurance premiums written each year in the United States. Insurance premiums are a direct function of the frequency and severity of accidents. In a world of driverless cars, where accidents are significantly curtailed, most of those premiums will go away. Sure, some car insurance would be needed, but the market might be reduced by 75 percent or more. Insurers make their profits on the float from their premium income, so plunging premiums spells doom for many insurers.

However, based on numerous conversations, it's clear that insurance-industry executives mostly just roll their eyes if asked to contemplate the implications of driverless cars. Even if driverless cars are possible, conventional wisdom goes, it will be decades before they are relevant. Therefore, there is little need to worry now.

Here's how insurers figure the math: Begin with the assumption that it will be years before the technology matures. Add several more years to sort out the regulatory complexities, including licensing and liability issues. Add some more years to gain consumer confidence. Then, given the long lifespan of cars, add another decade or more before driverless cars make up a significant percentage of the cars on the road.

---

86   Joseph B. White, "Unlocking the Secrets of a Car Thief," *Wall Street Journal*, July 10, 2012, http://online.wsj.com/article/SB100014240527023035677045775186530307307 54.html?grcc=88888Z0ZhpgeZ1Z0Z0Z0Z0&mod=WSJ_hpp_sections_lifestyle.

On top of that, the argument goes, even if the frequency of accidents goes down, the severity will go up—as measured in the cost to fix cars with all the cameras, sensors, radars, and so on, that are going into them. And, remember, even if you don't crash into someone else, someone else might well crash into you. So, it will be decades before anyone could even imagine giving up car insurance.

Besides, there might be no short-term cost to being wrong. Fewer accidents would just mean fewer claims, and therefore greater profits, until enough actuarial data proved that driverless technology delivered the conjectured savings and forced premiums down.

Thus, the prevailing attitude is probably much like that of Glenn Renwick, CEO of Progressive Insurance, as expressed during Progressive's February 2013 earnings call:

> "The technology to do an autonomous car has been around for a while. We're now seeing them; we'll see a lot of talk about them. The real issue is exactly how they are able to be part of the fleet of vehicles on the road in America, and that is probably not something that need keep anyone awake for quite some time."[87]

In fact, it's time for insurance executives to lose a little sleep. For one thing, far-off doomsdays have a way of sneaking up on you. The dangers to newspapers, music companies, book publishers, photography, and other industries were well understood for years before crises arose—yet plenty of companies were still caught by surprise. The more tangible issue is that Google's driverless car program has started a technology arms race across the auto industry that will hasten the disruption to insurers. If auto industry executives and boards of direc-

---

87   "Progressive Management Discusses Q4 2012 Results—Earnings Call Transcript," *Seeking Alpha*, February 28, 2013, http://seekingalpha.com/ article/1234441-progressive-management-discusses-q4-2012-results-earnings-call-transcript.

tors were not focused on this transition before, they're paying attention now. Most automakers are racing to differentiate their premium models with intelligent driver-assist functions like smart cruise control, accident avoidance, and crash monitoring and reporting. These efforts will hasten consumer trust in driverless technology and accelerate the proliferation of the technology throughout all car models. As an example, Volvo, an automaker known for safety but relatively small in terms of global sales, predicts that it will be able to eliminate crashes altogether for anyone driving one of its cars by 2020.[88] If tiny Volvo can aspire to this audacious goal, what might Big Auto be able to do?

The Volvo approach will hasten disruption for insurers because most accidents happen in congested traffic. Guy Fraker, a former director of enterprise innovation at State Farm Insurance, argues that even a 25 percent adoption of incremental driverless technology such as smart cruise control and crash avoidance would significantly relieve congestion and reduce the number of congestion-related accidents.[89] His analysis is consistent with the forecast that one large insurer shared with us. That forecast estimated that a 20 percent adoption rate of incremental driver-assist technology might result in significant enough reductions in accidents to trigger material reductions in premiums.

In other words, insurers will feel the effects of driverless technology long before fully autonomous cars become ubiquitous. The industry may well have to start making strategic choices in the next few years.

Auto insurers need to face this doomsday scenario and ask themselves: Why would anyone need car insurance in a world without accidents (or with a small fraction of today's number)? What if a company springs up that starts selling insurance to the manufacturers to be

---

88   Viknesh Vijayenthiran, "Volvo Predicts Crash-Proof Cars by 2020," *Motor Authority,* January 31, 2013, http://www.motorauthority.com/news/1082032_volvo-predicts-crash-proof-cars-by-2020-video.

89   Interview with Guy Fraker.

bundled with cars, locking up the manufacturers for the time when cars go driverless and the manufacturers, not the drivers, are responsible for insurance? What if automakers leverage their current warranty operations to offer insurance themselves?

Insurers need to start with a clean sheet of paper and perhaps reimagine themselves from the standpoint of the individual customer. In other words, companies could set aside traditional notions of demographic groups, geographic groupings, agents' territories, and so on. Companies could let each customer interact with her insurer in whatever way she wanted and then figure out how to price accordingly. Basically, companies could decide that customers want what they want, when they want it, and would work around that stark reality.

Perhaps a company could insulate itself from disruptive changes in today's massive auto insurance market by leveraging its current position into what might be called "all perils" insurance. Rather than offer many different types of insurance that provide varying forms of protection—auto, life, homeowners, workers' comp, and so on—why not just sell a single policy that covers all risks to a person's life and property based on age, assets, and all the personal behaviors that can be monitored easily via sensors and smartphones?

Focusing on auto insurance, maybe people want to point to a destination on their smartphone map and buy just the insurance to get there, based on how far they'll go, whether they're in a hurry, what time it is, and what route they intend to take. They might set a monthly insurance budget and thus want to be notified when the price dropped below a certain level, perhaps at the end of rush hour. They would allow for monitoring of their car to ensure that they acted as they said they would when buying the insurance. Local agents might still have some sort of role in the customer-based redesign, but they would no longer function as what Tom Wilson, CEO of Allstate, has referred to as "human modems."

Inventing the future would also entail looking at the future technological context beyond driverless cars that will create lots of other opportunities to win customers—or have them stolen.

For instance, insurers might use emergent knowledge drawn from external sources, such as social network activity, financial transactions, and online databases, to anticipate when purchasers are looking for new cars and market to them. Leading-edge insurers might poach customers nearing renewal dates with competitors. Emergent knowledge made available because the "connected" car of the future will always be communicating with the cloud will let smart insurers focus very specifically on the risk for an individual, rather than relying on averages based on age, gender, and a few other fairly crude indicators. That new knowledge will change underwriting models and could let an insurer lure away the lowest risks, leaving other insurers with potentially disastrous levels of claims. As one insurance CEO told us, "Insurers with better information make smarter underwriting decisions and slaughter those with less; that's the nature of the business."

Having gone through the Think Big exercises, insurers would then have to figure out how to Start Small if they want to be on the winning side of change.

Getting the finance operations to step aside during the early stages of innovation would be especially hard, given that actuarial tables and number-crunching are at the core of insurers. So, the insurers should have already started managing the finance arm by getting them involved not only in the doomsday scenario, but also the work on the clean sheet of paper. If the finance people themselves generate spreadsheets that show the company's existing businesses getting crushed or, in a kinder world, transforming because of an innovation and dominating the competition, finance will be more willing to bide its time while small experiments are carried out.

How to get everyone on the same page would depend on the culture of the company. The biggest problems will be at companies that use agents, who are generally set up as independent businesses and thus look out for themselves even more than employees do. In other words, it may simply not be possible to get agents to go along with the kinds of technological changes that the insurer wants to pursue, because those changes surely involve less of a role for agents.

Insurers need to try, so, as part of a look at all their cultural impediments, they should understand agents as deeply as they can and write "future histories" that explain how attempts at change might be stopped by agent resistance, perhaps buttressed by attempts to form unions and to draw on state laws protecting agencies. (We've used future histories to galvanizing effect at one large insurer.)

The key, though, will be in setting up a basket of killer options. A company could try to define a new relationship with agents, but there's enough uncertainty that mistakes would be made, and agents would surely resist. So, the company needs to feel its way toward possible changes, while taking as little risk as possible. That means setting up options.

One option might be to pick two or three agencies and, with minimal investment, turn them into "agencies of the future." Perhaps the insurer would take over all the processing work, saving costs by getting clients to do as much as possible online. The insurer might combine the agencies' data with corporate sources and types of emergent knowledge to do a far more sophisticated analysis than the agencies themselves could in terms of identifying potential clients, selling new services to existing clients, and even, perhaps, understanding just what a client wants. The insurer would then feed its insights back to the local agents for action. The insurer might also generate content that agents could use on social media sites to attract customers or interact with them in helpful ways. Basically, the insurer would be using technology to gain all the advantages of centralized data analysis and processing, plus all possible economies of scale, while maintaining the local touch.

Because the insurer would be taking on considerable additional work, it would lower commission percentages while hoping that enough new business would arise that the agencies would come out ahead on revenue and profit. If the agency of the future concept works, the insurer would be able to showcase it and talk to its whole agent force based on real numbers, not hypothetical ones. Agents would still be skeptical, but much less so.

Given that agents aren't the whole game, even at companies that use them, insurers also might set up options based on likely answers to intriguing questions. For instance, how will customer behavior and expectations evolve in the face of new technologies (keeping in mind that it isn't just other insurers that will set expectations, but also Amazon, FedEx, and others that set broad perceptions about how consumers can expect to be treated)? Or, what if insurers could have perfect information about customers? How would that change how insurers target, market to, and serve customers? How would it change their approach to regulators? How would competitors react?

As we've said, the idea would be to keep the number of options manageable. Otherwise, senior management couldn't pay enough attention, and even the successes would get lost. At the same time, there need to be enough so that, with minimal investment, it would be possible to start removing the uncertainty about how the future could look.

With the basket of killer options defined, it would be time to turn to our third step—Learn Fast—so companies could start identifying the winners, bring them to scale, and reap the benefits of continued success.

PHASE THREE:
LEARN FAST

~ *Rule 7*
A Demo Is Worth a Thousand Pages of a Business Plan

In the late 1990s, following the publication of *Unleashing the Killer App*, we were surprised to find that some of our partners were selling significant engagements to develop detailed business plans for killer apps. Knowing that too much early financial analysis could kill a promising idea, we suspected that it wouldn't be possible to accurately predict the course of a successful killer app at the earliest stages, either. But our partners said they were just providing what the client wanted—lots of detail—and consulting firms rarely turn down big fees to deliver what clients want.

As it happens, those business plans didn't survive first contact with the market—to paraphrase what Helmuth von Moltke said about battle plans and first contact with the enemy. The analysis was done by very bright folks at our firm and vetted by executive teams at companies that are household names, so the problem wasn't the quality of the work. The problem is that the situation was inherently unpredictable. But many companies still spend months on plans that will soon be tossed away.

Some of the reason is simple overconfidence—people think they can predict the future far better than they can. Some of the reason is habit—planning is what big companies do. New initiatives can't typically proceed without detailed business plans and reams of confirming spreadsheets.

Some of the reason, though, relates to an insidious problem that shows the need to reframe the whole process of going from idea to product or service. The problem is that, once a project gains any momentum, it becomes unstoppable. Even a green light for an early phase tends to turn an idea into a conventional development process: a long march where the only acceptable outcome is to get a product to market. As a result, people do all the analysis they can up front, however imprecise, and the result becomes The Plan.

To take a big, very public example, look at ethanol. It started out, in the United States, as an experiment in the early 1970s to see whether corn could produce a fuel that would replace gasoline. The answer was a resounding no. Among other problems, it actually takes more energy to produce a gallon of ethanol from corn than the fuel provides to a car. Yet here we are, four decades later, and ethanol has not only not been killed as a fuel additive or substitute but is actually legally required to provide roughly 20 percent of our fuel supply. The requirement stands even when drought drives corn prices sky high and feedlots become desperate for the corn that is going into fuel.

In the case of ethanol, the problem is farm state senators, who won't let the ethanol subsidies end, because they're invested in keeping corn prices high, benefiting their constituents and—most importantly—getting reelected. But every company has the equivalent of farm state senators. Once a project gets any kind of momentum, some people work as hard as possible to keep it going.

Many companies think they solve the problem of staying nimble by setting up pilot projects to validate concepts before they're rolled out nationally. But pilots aren't the answer, either, at least not on their own. Once something gets anointed as a "pilot," it's no longer an option—it's the destination. There are typically no graceful ways to kill a pilot, and even course corrections are too hard to make. Systems such as software have all been done at the production level, with the assumption that the pilot will work and will need to be quickly rolled out at scale. Changes are seen as a sign of defeat, and digging into production code can be complicated. Besides, problems at the pilot stage often get hidden. A pilot is very public, and some senior people have a strong interest in success, so they may work behind the scenes and use their connections to make it successful. We watched a client be all over a pilot in a single state, so thoroughly covering the pilot with senior-management attention that the client learned little before initiating a national rollout. The executives knew what they were doing, but they couldn't help themselves. They were so invested in the success of the pilot.

The Global Hawk demonstrates the potential problems with moving too quickly to the pilot stage—or, more precisely, to the pilot-less stage, given that the Global Hawk is a major program to use drones to conduct high-altitude reconnaissance in dangerous areas, in lieu of the U2 planes that pilots have been flying since the 1950s.

Using drones makes a lot of sense. Although it has been years since an enemy has even tried to shoot down a U2—the super-high-tech spy plane that flies above 70,000 feet and that has extensive anti-missile capabilities—sending a person so high in the atmosphere is inherently dangerous and expensive. Replacing the pilots and their aging U2s (mostly built in the 1980s) with drones would seem likely to save huge amounts of money and possibly lives.

Once Predator drones, which fly at low altitude and may carry missiles, showed success in conducting surveillance and attacking certain targets in the wars in Iraq and Afghanistan, pressure built to field a high-altitude drone. Northrup Grumman quickly produced a pilot, with the notion that kinks would be worked out along the way. But the basic design was set, and tinkering didn't fix the problems that, inevitably, appeared in an aircraft that costs more than $200 million each. The drones worked, and some were deployed, but the sensors weren't as good as those on the U2, and the drones caused maintenance nightmares. Of the eleven deployed in Iraq and Afghanistan, three crashed. In theory, it costs $220 million more a year to operate a U2 than a Global Hawk; in practice, the Global Hawks have been far more expensive. In 2012, on the third version of the Global Hawk, the Air

Force said it would halt production and wait for the fourth version, to see if that version finally operated as hoped. The Air Force actually said it would turn back to Congress the money that had been designated for purchases of the third version of the Global Hawk.[90] A high-profile, multibillion-dollar project flopped because it was rushed into the pilot stage too quickly.

The solution is to rephrase the issue. There needs to be less planning and more testing. The only way to accomplish that is to defer the pilot stage and stay in the prototyping phase much longer than most companies do.

The difference between a prototype and a pilot is that there's no possibility or expectation that a prototype will turn into the final version of the product or service. Prototypes are just tests to explore key questions, such as whether the technology will work, whether the product concept will meet customer needs, or whether customers will prefer it over the competitive alternatives.

The early prototypes should be all chewing gum and baling wire. They shouldn't have hardened processes or the people required to go live. Yet they should provide real insight that informs further development. Each stage of prototyping should minimize costs and maximize flexibility. To borrow a term from computer programming, new products and services should be explored using "late binding"; they should take final form as late as possible, based on the most up-to-date learnings that can be generated.

At Schwab, in the lead-in to the company's great, early successes with the Internet, executives talked about a hamster on a wheel. Schwab would test potential services by having people working behind the scenes answering questions, looking up information, and so on,

---

90   Congress decreed that the Air Force had to spend the allocated money. Killing a
      Department of Defense project may be even harder than killing ethanol.

running just as fast as their little (metaphorical) legs could go. Anything that didn't work or didn't resonate with customers was easily set aside. Only once Schwab had a sense of what customers truly wanted would it start building the capabilities into software.

Bob Lutz, legendary in the auto industry for producing cars that captured the imagination of certain sets of customers, used a process he called 9-3-1. In coming up with a new vehicle, he had three separate teams each produce three design concepts in sketches and small-scale clay models. The initial work was inexpensive, fast, and creative. Lutz and a few other senior product-development executives picked one concept from each team, which then produced a full-scale clay model. After some market research to resolve questions, Lutz and his team picked one for production.[91]

While Ray Kroc bought the rights to McDonald's from the McDonald brothers in the early 1960s with the clear intention of building the national and then international empire that has resulted, he paused long enough to test every aspect of the restaurant concept even though it had already been a rip-roaring success in Southern California—and it's a good thing he did. Among many other issues, he learned that french fries cooked in his test kitchen in Chicago bore no resemblance to the fries he had eaten in San Bernardino, California. He checked, double-checked and triple-checked to make sure he was following the exact process that the McDonald brothers used, but his fries still came out mushy. Nobody was going to fall in love with those fries. After much experimentation, Kroc finally realized that climate was the issue. The McDonald brothers left their potatoes in open crates outdoors before slicing and frying them, and the potatoes dried out

---

91   Lutz, by the way, says driverless cars could be ubiquitous in twenty years. Morgan Korn, "All Cars Will Be Driverless in 20 Years," *Yahoo? Finance,* September 26, 2012, http://finance.yahoo.com/blogs/daily-ticker/cars-driverless-20-years-bob-lutz-133826028.html.

in the Southern California sun. That wasn't going to happen indoors in Chicago in winter, so Kroc had to figure out some way to dry the potatoes the right amount before he could start counting the billions served.

Pixar has made a religion of prototyping through what the company calls "story reels." The company doesn't just write a script; it creates storyboards that provide a sort of comic-book version of a prospective movie, then adds dialogue and music. The story reels cost almost nothing, compared with the fully animated versions of Pixar's movies, yet provide a great sense of how a story will flow and allow for problems to be spotted. The story reels can also be changed easily.

In the early days of the company, with *Toy Story 2*, the storyboards saved the day. The creative folks at Pixar could see they had a real problem: The story was too predictable. The main character, a cowboy doll named Woody, had to decide whether to escape a kidnapper who wanted to send him to a toy collector in Japan. But it was obvious that Woody was going to escape and return to Andy, the boy who owned him. After months of banging their heads against the wall, the creative folks tried several things, including having the cowgirl doll named Jessie try to talk Woody into going to Japan, because she'd been set aside by her little girl owner and wanted a new life there. The Pixar folks could see they finally had the drama they needed. Jessie was going to give Woody a heartrending choice. While the movie had initially been planned as straight-to-video, in the Disney tradition of pumping out watered-down versions of its stories, *Toy Story 2* was released in theaters. It was another enormous success and paved the way for all that followed at Pixar.[92]

Every regular review of progress on the prototypes should begin with a demo, much like what Pixar does with its storyboards. Our old friend and colleague Gordon Bell, who designed the first minicomputer while at Digital Equipment, likes to say that "one demo is worth

92   Ed Catmull, "How Pixar Fosters Collective Creativity," *Harvard Business Review*, September 2008, http://hbr.org/2008/09/how-pixar-fosters-collective-creativity/ar/1.

a thousand pages of a business plan," and that notion applies to every stage of prototyping. It's easy to get lost in talk of assets, competencies, and market segments. A demo makes an idea tangible in a way that no business plan ever will.

Prototypes and demos are part of what has made Apple products so successful. Steve Jobs and designer Jonathan Ive always used prototypes of products to drive their thinking. For example, early in the process of figuring out the right screen size for the iPad, Jobs and Ive had twenty models made in slightly varying sizes. These were laid out on a table in Ive's design studio, and the two men and their fellow designers would play with the models. "That's how we nailed what the screen size was," Ive said.[93]

Admittedly, it helps when you have a genius like Jobs playing with the devices, but even he couldn't envision everything. He needed something tangible. As he was quoted as saying in the biography by Walter Isaacson that came out shortly after Jobs's death in 2011, "You have to show me some stuff, and I'll know it when I see it."

Apple's experience with the iPad highlights an irritating aspect of prototyping: It doesn't fit neatly into budgets, deadlines, and other normal aspects of conventional business planning. Apple worked on iPad prototypes for years until Jobs felt that all the technology issues were worked out and that the market was ready. But, the pot odds were hugely in favor of continuing while the cost of additional prototyping was minimal, so Apple kept paying to keep the option alive. (Prolonged prototyping can have unexpected side benefits, too. At one point, Jobs and others hit upon the idea that, while the technology wasn't ready for them to produce a tablet computer, it was ready to be turned into a phone.)

---

93   Walter Isaacson. *Steve Jobs.* New York: Simon & Schuster, 2011. The context was ads, not products, but the principle is the same. James Vincent, the ad executive whom Jobs was addressing, was unimpressed. He said, "Oh, great, let me write than on my brief for my creative people: I'll know it when I see it." But Jobs, of course, won the argument.

The attention to prototyping pervaded the entire Apple design process—even when Jobs was not involved. As a rule, Apple designers created ten different mock-ups of any new feature being considered. These mock-ups were exact demonstration images—down to the very pixel—for every single screen and feature that a user would see. The ten ideas were then narrowed down to three options, which were then further refined until the design team chose the one winning option.[94]

Oh, and there's one more thing about demos: They need to be constructed from the customer point of view. The demos must be created so that executives and others can play with them as though they're actual customers, with minimal guidance about how to use them. After all, customers don't have an expert guide answering their every question in the real world. If demos aren't done from the customer point of view, the customer can get lost—and even minor issues may matter a lot in terms of customer behavior.

There's a new system at Thomson Reuters called Eikon, which was supposed to be a Bloomberg killer. Thomson Reuters spent years and more than $1 billion building the system, adding all the features that traders said they wanted and going beyond what Bloomberg offered. But Thomson Reuters misunderstood how traders would use the system. Among other things, Thomson Reuters valued the private chat function on their Bloomberg terminals. Traders wouldn't say how much they valued it. Maybe they didn't even know. They mostly used chat to tell each other tasteless jokes, so they certainly didn't need it. But traders did value the function, and they resisted the Thomson Reuters terminal partly because that function wasn't there. A prototype placed in the hands of a few dozen traders could have spotted the weakness early—before the project leaders and, eventually, the CEO lost their jobs.[95]

94   Alain Breillatt, "You Can't Innovate Like Apple," *Pragmatic Marketing*, http://www.pragmaticmarketing.com/resources/You-Cant-Innovate-Like-Apple.

95   Greg Lambert, "Glocer Steps Down: Has Thomson Reuters Become the Next General Motors?": *Three Geeks and a Law Blog, December 2, 2011*, http://www.geeklawblog.com/2011/12/glocer-steps-down-has-thomson-reuters.html

Just about every company argues that they put the customer first. We once saw an org chart for AT&T that put the customer at the top and the CEO at the bottom. But just about every company also routinely claims to have the best people—a statistical impossibility. In fact, companies tend to do what's convenient for them. That's why, until relatively recently, retailers used price tags that were nearly impossible to remove, even though customers hated having to scrape the tags off and sometimes had to resort to using nail polish remover. That insular focus is why instructions for assembly can still be so bad—instructions are just an item to be checked off someone's to-do list; someone inspects the instructions, but he's surely an engineer who is intimately familiar with the product and could assemble it in his sleep. Companies that claim to love their customers construct customer-service systems that try very hard to make customers give up and go away. When a customer actually reaches a live person, she likely needs to know an account number or a confirmation number that has nothing to do with how she views the world—which is in terms of name, address, flight number and date, and so on.

Apple has shown the value of a radical emphasis on designing products that are intuitive and fun. But companies are far more likely to be like Sony, which has become known for having engineers design complicated products that will be loved by other engineers—but not by the rest of us. Explaining the difference, one analyst wrote: "Apple would never design a two-sided remote, touch screen with physical buttons on the front, full QWERTY keyboard on the back, of the complexity found in Sony's NSZ controllers. [Apple] also would limit the available functions to the things that users actually use, not just everything they could think of."[96]

---

96   Anthony Wing Kosner, "New Sony Google TV Set-Top Box Disappoints, Increases Desire for Apple TV," *Forbes*, June 25, 2012, http://www.forbes.com/sites/anthonykosner/2012/06/25/new-sony-google-tv-set-top-box-disappoints-increases-desire-for-apple-tv/

Doing demos at each step of the process that show how a product will work from a customer viewpoint and that let customers interact with a product will go a long way toward shaping products and services that customers will love.

Demos and prototypes also crystallize an understanding of how innovation will fare against the competition. When Bill Gates was CEO of Microsoft, he often spent the first half hour of a one-hour product review session asking the team what they'd heard about what competitors were doing, then discussed how Microsoft's efforts would do against the competition.

In most cases, you'll wind up doing several rounds of prototypes as you search for vulnerabilities and reduce key uncertainties about product viability. In rare cases, like the iPad, you might do many more rounds. The key is to remember that prototyping is simply an information-gathering process. You're looking for evidence of both potential success and failure, but all you want to learn is whether you know enough to kill the project, to move forward in a clear direction, or to continue exploring.

Remember the key point: Any clear information represents success, whether it suggests that an idea would succeed in the market or fail.

Killing high-aspiration projects is always difficult, even for the most analytical and disciplined companies. You need to be ready to do so, however, if the prototyping reveals some technological or market weakness that has no foreseeable solution. You might even want to start some low-cost, low-probability projects just so you can kill them in a way that shows your organization that projects can be killed and that association with a failed venture isn't toxic. You might also talk about "setting aside" projects, rather than killing them outright. The rationale could be that the iPad was repeatedly set aside yet became a blockbuster once the technology progressed enough.

If the results after a round of prototyping are still unclear, be very specific about what issues need to be explored. Then lather, rinse, repeat—until you've answered all the key questions.

Once you're confident that you're ready to exercise your option and proceed in a specific direction, you may be tempted to throw away all the prototypes and go straight to full production and rollout. Sometimes, your team will argue that you need to move fast or someone else will, but that can get you into trouble. Instead, this is the time to do a pilot.

Webvan rolled out its same-day delivery service in the late 1990s at great speed for fear that someone would beat it to the punch. The company granted a $1 billion contract to Bechtel to build its highly automated warehouses and expanded to ten cities almost immediately. But there were many problems that Webvan hadn't anticipated. The company hadn't understood how expensive it could be to deliver small orders to customers who weren't super near each other, how hard it is to park a van in a city long enough to make a delivery, or how bad traffic can be in rush hour. But it was all too late. Webvan had dispensed with prototypes and had moved through the pilot stage so fast that it didn't have time to learn much, let alone incorporate that knowledge into its national rollout. The company filed for bankruptcy less than two years after its launch.

By contrast, Amazon has been prototyping various aspects of same-day delivery for years now. Its Amazon Prime service learned that customers value free delivery. Numerous tests since then have experimented with how buying behaviors change if Amazon beats its promise of two-day delivery and delivers the product the next day. Now, in some markets, Amazon is delivering certain products the same day. It's also experimenting with dropboxes. If a customer isn't going to be home,

Amazon will deliver a product to the box at a nearby facility such as a convenience store. The company then e-mails a code to the customer, who can pick up the product at his convenience—in the process, saving Amazon the cost of a second or third attempt at home delivery.[97]

We obviously can't say just how Amazon will handle a pilot of same-day delivery, if it ever gets there, but it's handling the process just right to this point. It's making many small tests and learning a lot, delaying the day when it has to piece everything together into a commercial offering. Because Amazon is taking a prototyping-based approach, it will be very sophisticated about whatever it does.

So, be Amazon, not Webvan. Focus on prototyping that's set up so that the process is entirely about learning, not about The Plan. Test and test and test until you're sure you have all the potential problems addressed, even if the process takes years, and ideas have to be set aside multiple times, until technology and market conditions provide the right environment for a launch.

To bastardize Milton Friedman, there's no such thing as a free launch—so make sure you learn everything possible before committing yourself to one.

---

97   Farhad Manjoo, "I Want It Today: How Amazon's Push for Same-Day Delivery Will Destroy Local Retail," *Slate*, July 11, 2012, http://www.slate.com/articles/business/small_business/2012/07/amazon_same_day_delivery_how_the_e_commerce_giant_will_destroy_local_retail_.html?tid=sm_tw_button_toolbar.

~ *Rule 8*
Remember the Devil's Advocate

Setting up the right process for demos, prototypes, and pilots is crucial—but it's only half the battle when it comes to learning fast. The other half is making sure you ask the tough questions during the process and remain open to hearing uncomfortable answers.

That's why you need to call on your inner skeptic or empower an explicit devil's advocate. As Clayton Christensen has observed, "More often than not, failure in innovation is rooted in not having asked an important question, rather than having arrived at an incorrect answer."

Irving Janis, in his seminal work, *Groupthink,* laid out the types of questions that even the best decision-making groups tend not to ask. According to his research, groups

- Make an incomplete survey of objectives
- Take an incomplete survey of alternatives
- Fail to examine risks of the preferred choice
- Fail to reappraise initially rejected alternatives
- Make a poor search for information
- Show bias in processing information
- Fail to work out contingency plans

The way to minimize these common decision-making traps is to build tough questioning explicitly into your company's innovation process.

Philosophically, we recommend an approach akin to the devil's advocate that the Catholic Church used for centuries to safeguard canonization, the process by which the church declared someone to be a saint. In the Middle Ages, the church began appointing a person whose role was to take a skeptical view. He worked in concert with other investigators, but his role was to critically assess all evidence and presumptions and lay out all reasonable arguments for why the prospective saint should be denied recognition. While the name "devil's advocate" is a bit challenging, two things should be noted. First, the formal name of the office was *promoter fidel*, or "promoter of the faith." In other words, the idea was to build the church, not to be punitive. Second, the office was effective. Since Pope John Paul II abolished the office in the early 1980s, the rate of canonization has increased by a factor of more than twenty, amid reports that church officials have ignored unflattering evidence.

Applied to business, the devil's advocate is an individual or group whose role is to assess all critical assumptions, key forecasts, and other make-or-break aspects of a potential killer app. The goal is not to inter- ject an abject naysayer into the decision-making process, but rather to drive at the answer that best serves the long-term success of the organization. Nor is the goal to relegate the task of critical thinking to the devil's advocate. Instead, the devil's advocate process serves as a safety net, and, because everyone knows that tough questions are forthcoming, they'll be more likely to confront them.

We may all be alive today because of a devil's advocate. The Kennedy administration team that botched the Bay of Pigs in 1961 turned around and, with the same key players, performed masterfully while tiptoeing on the brink of nuclear war during the Cuban missile crisis in 1962. The key difference was a devil's advocate. President Kennedy, having learned from the Bay of Pigs fiasco, asked his brother Robert to serve as a devil's advocate during the missile crisis. Robert was to question all assumptions and challenge all plans, even if put forward by people with great expertise. He had both the standing and the thick skin needed for the role and performed admirably. Among other things, he challenged an assertion by General Curtis LeMay, the Air Force chief of staff, that the United States could bomb Cuba without fear of retaliation by the Soviet Union. Instead, the Kennedy administration adopted a firm policy but gave the Soviet Union a way out short of war. The Soviets withdrew. Nuclear war was averted. We're alive.

In retrospect, it sounds crazy to think that the Soviets wouldn't have retaliated. They would have had to save face somehow. History shows that Che Guevara, Fidel Castro's right-hand man, argued furiously for an attack on the United States. Imagine if the Americans had bombed Cuba and provided a provocation.

But the assertion by LeMay was the kind of statement that went unchallenged during the Bay of Pigs—he claimed, for instance, that the attacking force couldn't be linked to the United States (even though planes with US insignia supported the attack) and that fighters could melt into the hills if the assault failed (even though the attack point had moved and was actually miles away from the hills, with nearly impassable marshes in the way).

LeMay's assertion about how the Soviet Union would act is also the kind of statement that can get made in the executive suite and lead to a doomed strategy. The statement won't be contradicted either because the complex psychology of teams has created groupthink or because people are reluctant to challenge the CEO or some other powerful executive.

Look at the decision by Blue Circle Cement to sell lawn mowers in the 1990s. The executive team at Blue Circle, the fifth-largest cement company in the world at the time, somehow convinced itself that it wasn't really in the cement business; it was in the home business. Homes have lawns, so Blue Circle diversified into making lawn mowers, among other things. Of course, the company didn't know the first thing about lawn mowers, and its cement customers had no interest in buying lawn mowers from Blue Circle. The company soon filed for bankruptcy protection and was purchased by Lafarge in 2001.

In our research for *Billion Dollar Lessons*, we looked for strategies that often led to failures, such as Blue Circle's ill-advised move into a supposedly adjacent market. We found a number of them. We also saw patterns that cut across the perilous strategies—in particular, that companies often overestimated the benefits of scale and underestimated the complexities that could come with scale if, for instance, a cement company tried to grow by selling home products rather than just making more cement. The most striking finding from the 2,500 major failures, though, had to do with the failure to ask tough questions. We found that almost half the strategies that led to huge writedowns or to bankruptcy proceedings over a quarter of a century were so clearly wrong that they could have been prevented if the organization had taken an objective second look to vet them.

It doesn't take much to see that a cement company has no business selling lawn mowers. Or that Avon's core asset has historically been its door-to-door sales force, not a "culture of caring," even though that's what the executive team concluded in the mid-1980s, leading to the ill-fated purchase of retirement centers and a maker of medical equipment and a $545 million write-off just a few years later. Or that Sony shouldn't shell out billions of dollars for a movie studio in the hopes that people would not only notice that they were watching a Sony movie but care enough that, when watching at home, they would want to use a Sony TV attached to a Sony VCR.[98] Or that Kodak shouldn't spend half a billion dollars developing a camera, the Advantix, that was fully digital but that still required users to buy film and have prints made.

---

98   Sony bought Columbia Pictures for $3.4 billion in 1989, then took a $2.7 billion write-down on the investment in 1994, yet two decades later is still pursuing the same sort of synergy that led to the ill-fated purchase. The mind reels.

Every company can use some version of a devil's advocate to head off similar problems while attempting innovation—but the devil's advocate is, if you will, in the details.

The first issue, of course, is that you have to commit to the process. And you need to do so at the beginning. Everyone has to agree on when a devil's advocate will be involved, whether insiders or outsiders will play the role, and how the role will play out. If you wait until you're in the heat of a moment, when a decision is being made on a real, live innovation, everyone will have chosen sides. Those who want the idea to go to market will resist a devil's advocate, for fear it will slow or kill the project. Those who oppose the idea will insist on a devil's advocate. Both sides will try to tilt the playing field in their favor. The only way to get everyone on board is to set the rules before anyone knows whether they're for or against a particular project—when we've made presentations in front of groups of directors of Fortune 100 companies, they always say this point is key, that the process has to be defined ahead of time. The processes have to be specified in detail, too. As things stand, many companies like the theory of devil's advocacy but never implement it.

The second issue is that the goal of devil's advocacy must be framed correctly. It can't be about killing projects or even identifying flaws. Otherwise, the process becomes a game of gotcha. Some people will win, but others will lose. The process will generate so much tension that people will shy away from it. Instead, the devil's advocate needs to be about reducing uncertainty, about learning—even if information that is unearthed discredits the idea. The devil's advocate helps bring to the surface issues that might otherwise be ignored and ensures that issues, once raised, are addressed and not just glossed over as a project gains momentum. Everyone can get behind those goals.

The third issue is that, even though we write about devil's advocacy as our final rule, it should be applied throughout the innovation process. It makes sense, for instance, to assign someone the role to make sure that projections for potentially disruptive technologies go well into the future and are appropriately aggressive, rather than just being snapshots of where things stand today. It makes sense to have a devil's advocate challenge whether you've actually laid out a true doomsday scenario or are just considering a sort-of-bad scenario that obscures both problems and opportunities. It can be especially important to have a devil's advocate involved in getting everyone on the same page because, as we've seen, the tendency is to gloss over potential objections to a new strategy, and cultural problems can torpedo almost any killer app. The devil's advocate should be asked to ensure that the future histories include truly bleak possibilities.

An effective devil's advocate frames the most important questions that need to be answered before a killer app should be attempted at scale. The advocate also guides the process, making sure that the right amount of uncertainty is reduced at each step. It would obviously be unfair to demand great precision and certainty about an idea at the earliest stage. After all, if something is a true killer app it's moving into new territory, where certainty doesn't yet exist. But, at each new step, greater precision should be demanded, and, by launch stage, you want confidence before you commit a bunch of money and put your reputation on the line.

At each step, the management team, working with the devil's advocate, also preserves the possibility of what one client calls a "graceful exit." A reasonably small percentage of the ideas put forward as possible killer apps should make it to market, and it's important to be able to stop them at the right time. People get attached to their projects, and corporations tend to treat the end of a project as a failure that tars participants, so extra effort needs to go into preserving an out. By focusing on reducing uncertainty, the devil's advocate provides an easy way to set aside projects—rather than declare them dead—until the right level of confidence is reached.

Different people can play the role of devil's advocate, based on circumstances. In some cases, depending on the personalities involved, you can simply appoint someone to act as devil's advocate. Be sure that everyone knows the person's role, so that she has license to challenge everything without messing up the group dynamics. And it's important to rotate the role, so no one person gets labeled a stick-in-the-mud and loses effectiveness. You may need to support the devil's advocate from time to time, perhaps by asking pointed questions yourself. Steve Jobs used to sometimes switch positions on strategic issues and argue passionately for something he didn't believe in, just to keep his team from settling in to a game of "let's guess what Steve is thinking." The more complicated a decision is, the more it makes sense to go through a more formal process and not rely on an insider as devil's advocate.

While every company is different, and while the devil's advocate concept can be implemented in many ways, we'll lay out our typical approach, so you can see how the idea might play out for you. This is the full-on process that we use for top executives at a large company, but the process can be scaled down for use at a division or even a local business that needs a double-check before proceeding with a risky innovation.

We begin an innovation process by interviewing executives in product, marketing, sales, and information technology functions about potentially disruptive technologies. We supplement those interviews with our own expertise on technology adoption curves and generate a memo on technologies to watch. We circulate that memo to the senior management team, then follow up with interviews about doomsday and clean-sheet-of-paper scenarios. Working with a point person, often the CEO herself, we synthesize a second time and generate a list of three to seven hypotheses about potential killer apps and how they might transform the company.

At this point, we hold a workshop that includes a dozen to twenty senior executives from the full array of corporate functions to assess, question, reconceptualize, and prioritize the potential ideas. The rationale for such heavy investment of senior-level resources is that if an idea is truly a killer app that could redefine the industry, then senior management needs to be involved from day one to shape and nurture it. Some companies also bring in other participants, perhaps rising stars, thought leaders, and outside experts.

Typically, we moderate the workshop using a process called SAST, for Strategic Assumptions Surfacing and Testing. SAST assumes that sufficient knowledge about possible innovation exists within the participating team—and it does. The issue is just changing the dynamics and pulling all that knowledge out of them. The process relies heavily on competition, both because it disarms people and gets them to speak freely and because competition sharpens ideas.

The process begins with the group divided into three or four teams and assigned a hypothesis on how to address a problem or opportunity. This is an important contrast to the traditional approach, which tries to evaluate a single strategy and thus constricts the conversation. By using multiple hypotheses, SAST brings into play any technology, competitor tactic, or customer issue that could redefine a market. By assigning hypotheses, the process liberates people from their predetermined positions and frees the conversation. (We typically assign the ranking executive a position she's known not to hold, so everyone sees that play acting is encouraged.)

The teams come up with a list of critical assumptions related to customers, competitors, technology, and so on that need to hold for their assigned approach to be the right strategy. Each team then ranks the conditions on two axes: how likely they are to be true and how crucial they are for the success of the assigned strategy.

The teams gather and share their positions, including charts that show where they rank their assumptions on importance and likelihood. People question and challenge one another in an informal way, always providing considerable insight. Each team is then assigned another team to contest and goes off to explore how to make that team's hypothesis look bad. In this preparation and in the public debate that follows, people bring to the surface all kinds of potential problems that tend to get ignored. Executives are both smart and competitive. They know everything there is to know about their industries. Once they're cut loose from having to defend a particular position and from having to worry about politics, they can be remarkably insightful. And, because they're going through SAST as a group, the insights aren't as dangerous as they can be in the normal course of business. It's possible to challenge the CEO and live to tell about it.

One client told us that the glow from the workshop carried over for months afterward. People found they could note potential problems that they would have previously glossed over because objections were politically incorrect. All they had to do was follow their remark by smiling and saying, "Just play acting. . . ."

The workshop has the added benefit of going a long way toward accomplishing the goals of Rules 4 and 5. In terms of killing all the finance guys, the workshop makes it clear that ideas are preliminary and can't be subjected to premature, detailed financial analysis. The workshop also demonstrates that senior management has bought into an array of potential ideas, providing important protection until real analysis can occur. The workshop helps to get everyone on the same page. People have challenged each other so pointedly that there's no doubt about, for instance, how long people assume it will take for an important change in the marketplace to occur. Work on Rules 4 and 5 needs to continue, especially in terms of keeping the management team headed in the same direction, but the workshop provides a great start and identifies many of the conflicts that might arise.

Once the results are summarized, the CEO (or general manager, or whomever) and his team generate a basket of killer options that will be explored. The initial questions that need to be addressed are identified, and the necessary resources are mobilized.

At this point, many organizations lapse into analysis-paralysis, so a steering committee meets at regular intervals to keep the team progressing and to set aside any projects that clearly won't pan out in the foreseeable future. The committee also keeps track of projects that, while not worth pursuing right away, could become viable after some change in technology or the market and reintroduces those projects into the innovation process at the appropriate time.

The committee needs to establish realistic but firm milestones that projects must meet if work on them is to continue. With projects that might have a near-term impact, the committee should meet every month or so. More typically, killer apps will play out over a longer term, given their far-reaching implications, so quarterly meetings are often sufficient.

Beyond the milestones, companies can use any number of other techniques to provide a sense of urgency. For instance, when Regina Dugan ran the incredibly successful US Department of Defense's Defense Advanced Research Projects Agency (DARPA), she never let a researcher stay more than two years. In fact, each researcher's ID badge listed the date his DARPA employment would end. People were constantly reminded that they had a limited time to make an impact.

In setting milestones, we use a diagnostic process called the RWW screening framework, which asks three questions.[99] The R stands for "Is it real?" In other words, what are the chances that the killer app we're envisioning can be made and address the needs of a sizable market? The first W stands for "Can we win?" That leads to questions about whether the product can beat the competition and whether the

---

99   George Day, "Is It Real? Can We Win? Is It Worth Doing?: Managing Risk and Reward in an Innovation Portfolio," *Harvard Business Review*, December 2007, http://hbr.org/2007/12/is-it-real-can-we-win-is-it-worth-doing-managing-risk-and-reward-in-an-innovation-portfolio/.

company can effectively bring it to market. The second *W* stands for "Is it worthwhile?" That leads to questions about whether there are sufficient profits to be made and how well the product fits with the company's overall strategy.

The RWW screening framework dovetails well with the iterative development and constant testing approach because it's not a one-and-done diagnostic. The same questions can be asked at different stages of learning, with the difference being the level of detail required of the answers. On the date of the innovation workshop, it's enough for the group to rely on back-of-the-envelope calculations and their experience and intuition that a killer app might be real and worthwhile and that the company can win. After several rounds of prototyping, more hard numbers, less intuition, and a thorough demonstration of technical viability are required. By the time you're ready to consider investing real money and going with a pilot, you need detailed market research, customer validation, modeling, financial analysis, and technical validation.

Other processes can work, too. The key is to stage the milestones to ensure progress, ask tough questions, and preserve graceful exits.

Toward the end of the product-development process or before the finalization of any strategic transaction (if the implementation is via an acquisition or partnership), we stage a rigorous "last-chance" review. This review offers an opportunity to step back and make sure that all the concerns that have been raised along the way have been addressed. If everything has gone well up to this point, the review will be a final opportunity to build consensus and ensure that everyone is on the same page. The review might also identify implementation-related problems that might surface and help everyone be better prepared if they do.

The last-chance review is particularly important in situations where acquisitions are involved. In the course of assessing specific acquisitions, dealmakers can get caught up in the desire to complete the deal, sometimes making unstated compromises, or even losing the connection with the motivating strategy. The review brings a fresh perspective to potential issues, ensuring that potential red flags are articulated and examined.[100]

Starbucks shows what can happen to even a super successful CEO and a great company when the review process is circumvented. In early 2008, Howard Schultz tasted a drink in a small, northern Italian town that he described as "a sweet, smooth, cold Italian-made beverage that was not ice cream or sorbet or a smoothie but—whether mixed with fruit, milk or yogurt—tasted absolutely delicious and like nothing else available in the United States."[101] Back-of-the-envelope calculations indicated that the product could provide Starbucks with profit margins of 70 percent, and Schultz felt a great sense of urgency. The company had hit enough problems that he had just returned as CEO, and the weakening economy was making matters worse, so Schultz decided to fast-track the beverage, called Sorbetto, and bring it to market in the summer of 2008. Only after hundreds of stores were decorated for a broad rollout of Sorbetto did the problems emerge. Pricing tests suggested a margin of 16 percent to 24 percent, not 70 percent. Sorbetto required specialized machines for mixing the drinks, an unforeseen expense. Worse, the machines took baristas an hour and a half to clean at the end of each day—baristas hated Sorbetto. [102]

---

100   For a more in-depth discussion of process safeguards and other planning techniques, see *Billion Dollar Lessons.*

101   Howard Schultz. *Onward: How Starbucks Fought for Its Life Without Losing Its Soul.* New York: Rodale Books, 2011.

102   Ibid.

If the situation at Starbucks was anything like what we've seen with many of our clients, plenty of people knew of the problems, but there was no devil's advocate process to make sure they surfaced in time for them to be addressed. With no time left in the summer of 2008, Schultz addressed the margin issue by raising the price, launched the product, and hoped. But Starbucks abandoned Sorbetto almost immediately.

By contrast, Procter & Gamble shows that even a huge, bureaucratic business can innovate successfully if it uses a devil's advocate. The company had identified an opportunity for a skin cream for what it called a "masstige" market—a portmanteau of "mass" and "prestige." P&G considered numerous possibilities, including spending billions of dollars on an acquisition. The company also looked at extending an existing product, Oil of Olay, to fill the opportunity. That was a challenge. The product was so thoroughly identified with older women that it was nicknamed "Oil for Old Ladies." But, using a home-grown process very like the devil's advocate, P&G kept identifying issues that needed to be resolved and kept addressing them with small tests, rather than letting executives rely on experience or intuition.

For instance, the development team tested three premium price points: $12.99, $15.99, and $18.99. They found, to their surprise, that they sold the most units at the highest price. At that $18.99 price, customers were actually crossing over and buying Oil of Olay in grocery and discount stores rather than buying a higher-priced product in department stores. The high price sent a message of luxury but still looked like a great value.

"These differences were quite fine," wrote A.G. Lafley, CEO of Procter & Gamble at the time. "Had the team not focused so carefully on building and applying robust tests for multiple price points, the findings might never have emerged."

He said P&G would have been happy with a global skin care brand generating $1 billion in annual sales, but in less than a decade the Olay brand surpassed $2.5 billion in annual sales.[103]

That's a pretty good argument for a devil's advocate.[104]

103 A. G. Lafley, Roger L. Martin, Jan W. Rivkin, and Nicolaj Siggelkow, "Bringing Science to the Art of Strategy," *Harvard Business Review,* September 2012, http://hbr.org/2012/09/bringing-science-to-the-art-of-strategy/ar/6.

104 Although Lafley retired as CEO in 2010, he was asked to return in May 2013.

~ *Case Study*
Are Hospitals DOA?

oogle isn't just developing its driverless cars. Employees take the cars almost everywhere—or, if you prefer, are taken just about everywhere by the half-dozen prototypes. The company makes employees use their own prototypes so they're fully, often painfully, aware of the problems. The term of art in Silicon Valley is that Google employees "eat their own dog food."

Making almost a religion of the Learn Fast principle that emphasizes the importance of demos, Google employees build an awful lot of prototypes. For Google, the whole point is to learn as quickly as possible, even though many efforts will end up heading down blind alleys and could be considered waste. With the driverless car, for instance, Google obviously has no intention of trying to turn its prototypes into production models. Google is just learning as much as it can about what works and what doesn't.

One of Google's tenets is that data beat intuition. Google also stresses the need for a common platform, so that everyone's iterations can be tested and evaluated in the same way and so Google can have a stream of data that everyone agrees on—nobody is entitled to her own data.

By contrast, we're not aware that Google has anything resembling a formal devil's advocate process. The company seems to rely on its engineering-driven culture, where people feel free to argue bluntly. That seems to be working well for now, though the lack of a devil's advocate could eventually lead to trouble.

To show how other companies should, likewise, Learn Fast and react to the prospects for radical changes in cars, we'll look at health care providers, in particular hospitals.

The obvious issue is that, if Google is right about what it can accomplish, hospitals will lose more than two million emergency-room patients a year in the United States alone because there will be radically fewer car accidents, and they'll lose 220,000 patients who would have needed overnight hospitalization. The reduction would take many tens of billions of dollars away from hospitals, so they have to test their way toward figuring out how real the threat is, how fast it might develop, and whether they can innovate by providing other services, such as preventive care, that would replace the disappearing revenue.

But the context for hospitals needs to be much broader. Beyond whatever Google and its car accomplish, developments in information technology could change the world of medicine—for instance, the smartphones that we all carry could provide medical apps, some of them profound. There will also, of course, be major advances in medical technology. In the United States, regulatory change associated with Obamacare, formally known as the Affordable Care Act, will have dramatic consequences—many of which will not be understood for years. Demographic changes such as the aging population and widespread afflictions such as obesity are increasing the complexity of care. At the same time, health care costs are rising too fast and putting too much of a strain on government financing. As a consequence, people are finally facing the fact that a fee-for-service model makes little sense. Health care should be designed for the health of us patients and shouldn't provide incentives based on how many treatments are ordered. Ideally, health care prevents disease, yet there is currently almost no profit in prevention; all the profit is in treatment.

The current system is clearly unsustainable. Hospitals are simply too complicated and inefficient. They were designed to be all things to all people. Costs were a nearly forbidden topic in the design, on the theory that all that mattered was giving patients the best care. Now, technology and regulatory changes are paving the way for such a radically different future that hospitals must change or lose. Without a new course, hospitals will lose their central place in medicine. Many will disappear.

Some of the technological change springs from advances in medical technologies and techniques that extend beyond the six electronic megatrends we've been discussing—mobile devices, social media, cameras, sensors, cloud computing, and emergent knowledge. For instance, greater experience in certain high-profit surgeries, such as hip replacements, means that they're moving to facilities that specialize in a certain type of elective surgery and that can be both better and less expensive than a general-purpose hospital. As medical equipment shrinks and becomes less expensive, much of the lab work and many of the big diagnostic machines will move downstream, out of hospitals and into doctors' offices and clinics. Eventually, equipment will move into people's homes.

But hospitals should still Think Big and through our six megatrends, because technologies such as ubiquitous cameras, cheap sensors, and tens of billions of mobile devices create further pressure for change by allowing for possibilities such as telemedicine. Many diagnoses and hospital care can be provided without the need for a hospital, and the trend has just started. In a few years, making an appointment for a traditional visit with a doctor may well feel like going to a Blockbuster to pick up a VHS tape. Similar changes might be in store for hospitals.

Emergent knowledge will change hospitals by making public information about charges that was previously proprietary. A recent study, for instance, publicized vast differences in the cost of the same operation at neighboring hospitals. In the Sacramento area, one hospital charged $48,507 for a knee replacement; another charged $142,722.[105] In San Francisco, cholesterol tests can cost $18—or $317. An MRI of

---

[105] Cynthia H. Craft, "Hospital Surgery Prices Vary Widely," *Sacramento Bee*, July 13, 2012, http://www.sacbee.com/2012/07/13/4628254/hospital-surgery-prices-vary-widely.html.

the back can cost \$425—or \$2,591.[106] How would you like to be the hospital in Arizona that was raked over the coals in newspapers for charging a woman \$80,000 for antivenom when the same medicine was available across the border in Mexico for \$200? (The newspapers noted that, because of stricter testing and regulation in the United States, the hospital paid about \$7,000 for the medication, but the fact that the hospital charged "only" a \$73,000 markup didn't win the hospital much sympathy.)

Looking for emergent knowledge, the Heritage Provider Network is offering a \$3 million prize for an algorithm that will spot the patients most likely to wind up in a hospital soon, so they can be treated before they need expensive hospitalization. The hope is to take a big bite out of the \$30 billion in unnecessary hospitalization that occurs in the United States each year.[107]

Tremendous cost reductions due to emergent knowledge might also come through pharmacogenomics, the use of genetic information to predict whether a drug will help make a patient healthy or ill. For example, only 40 percent of patients respond to drugs used in the treatment of rheumatoid arthritis. The most popular of these drugs—Enbrel, Remicade, and Humira—also happen to be among the top-grossing drugs worldwide, with aggregate sales of nearly \$30 billion—meaning that almost \$18 billion could have been wasted on these drugs alone.[108] More generally, at least a third of the roughly \$300 billion spent per year on prescription drugs in the United States alone is wasted because

---

106 Kerry A. Dolan, "The Start-Up that Is X-Raying the Doctor Bills," *Forbes,* June 27, 2012, http://www.forbes.com/sites/kerryadolan/2012/06/27/the-startup-that-will-save-us-from-obamacare/.

107 Philip Fasano. *Transforming Health Care: The Financial Impact of Technology, Electronic Tools, and Data Mining.* Hoboken, NJ: John Wiley & Sons, 2013.

108 Andrew R. Harper and Eric J. Topol, "Box 1: Missed Opportunities in Top Grossing Drugs," *Nature Biotechnology,* 30, 1117–24 (2012), doi:10.1038/nbt.2424.

those drugs are either ineffective or dangerous to recipients.[109] While not all of these prescription costs flow through hospitals, more targeted drug use, based on genetic information, would take a big chunk out of hospital revenue.

If, as many speculate, patients or their families have to pay some percentage of the cost of most medical procedures, then people will have major incentives to put emergent knowledge to good use. They will push back in ways they don't now, either because they don't have the information or are insulated against astronomical fees because of current insurance practices.

A senior executive, speaking alongside us in front of a group of medical executives a few years ago, berated himself for not having questioned the doctors harder as his father was dying several weeks earlier. He let the doctors make what he called "heroic" efforts, even though his elderly father's cancer was so advanced that there was no hope of remission. He figures his father lived an extra week—but was either miserable or unconscious the whole time. The bill to the insurance company for that extra week came to a quarter of a million dollars. More than 10 percent of health care costs come in the final year of life, and much of that is spent at hospitals, so any change in how people think about prolonging life would have a major impact on hospitals.[110]

Given all the pressures and all the economic inefficiencies at hospitals, it's reasonable to think that competitors will keep pulling away the most profitable treatments. Hospitals, without a course change, will be cut down to the bare essentials. Emergency rooms will always be with us. Operating rooms need to be available in some sort of centralized spot, and intensive care units and maternity wards might stay based in hospitals. But that's about it. It's possible to imagine a future where every other type of care winds up distributed into clinics like those at Walgreens, specialty facilities, and the home.

---

109 Ibid.

110 Arthur Garson Jr. and Carolyn L. Engelhard, "The Economics of Dying," *Governing the States and Localities,* March 31, 2009, http://www.governing.com/topics/health-human-services/The-Economics-of-Dying.html.

We don't expect the apocalypse for hospitals to happen anytime soon. In fact, we keep in mind the traditional problem with predictions about technology: People tend to overestimate the predictions in the short run while underestimating in the long run. None other than Thomas Edison said in 1913 that traditional education was dead; his movie projectors were going to make teachers and textbooks obsolete.[111] Yet here we are a century later, with education still happening in much the same way. We think fundamental change is coming, just not as fast as (the enormously self-promotional) Edison would have had it. As people in Silicon Valley say, it's important to "never confuse a clear view with a short distance."

We assume that changes with hospitals will take years to be transformative. Many health care providers are invested in the current system. Many regulations, including Medicare reimbursements, favor hospitals, and regulations are always slow to change. Besides, many communities feel that having a hospital is a badge of honor and will look for ways to protect theirs. At the same time, we'd bet that the changes will be earth-shattering when they come, much more so than those with vested interests would be willing to hear at this point. When it does come, the change will likely be quick and catch many unaware, simply because that's the history with killer apps.

We also know that it's always better to see what's coming in time to get out of the way. If we ran a hospital company, we'd start to Think Big by investigating the technology context. That's because technology is not only a disruptive force but is a key enabler to address the other forces, such as regulatory demands, demographic changes, and evolving standards of care.

---

111 Michael Hiltzik, "Who Really Benefits from Putting High-Tech Gadgets in Classrooms?" *Los Angeles Times*, February 4, 2012, http://articles.latimes.com/2012/feb/04/business/la-fi-hiltzik-20120205.

We'd learn about the latest technologies going into "the medical house" (a term that has actually been around since at least 1967 and refers to technologies that let the elderly and those with chronic medical conditions be monitored and counseled continually without leaving home). We'd look into the possibilities created by mobile devices and sensors to basically give everyone a medical house that they could take with them wherever they go.

In addition, we'd put considerable effort into staying on top of technology that, beyond the "house," digitizes the human. Just a couple of examples: the everyheartbeat project, which is trying to capture every beat of every person's heart, so doctors and researchers can learn what signals an impending heart attack and can find ways to get people to a doctor in time;[112] or those working on a smartphone app that could perform an eye refraction and send the image to an optometrist, who would have glasses made.[113] More generally, we'd pay attention to what Eric Topol calls the "perfect storm" of digital technologies allowing us to "illuminate the human black box." Topol, a noted cardiologist and academic director of Scripps Health, argues, "We can dissect, decode and define individual granularity at the molecular level, from womb to tomb."[114] Many in the medical profession are skeptical, but a key part of thinking big is to stay on top of dramatic claims—when they come from credible sources like Topol.

We'd make sure to understand the road map for medical technology that has the potential to threaten important streams of revenue. This includes high-priced investments that could escalate the medical arms race, like the new proton therapy treatments centers that can cost

---

112 Ariel Schwartz, "Using Big Data to Predict Your Potential Heart Problems," *Fast Company*, http://www.fastcoexist.com/1679654/using-big-data-to-predict-your-potential-heart-problems

113 Ron Winslow, "The Wireless Revolution Hits Medicine," *Wall Street Journal*, February 14, 2013, http://online.wsj.com/article/SB10001424052702303404704577311421888663472.html?mod=wsj_share_tweet#

114 Eric Topol. *The Creative Destruction of Medicine: How the Digital Revolution Will Create Better Health Care.* New York: Basic Books, 2012.

upward of $200 million to build. At the other extreme are the fruits of constant miniaturization, like the handheld ultrasound machines that sell for less than $10,000, as opposed to traditional cart-based ones that cost $250,000.

Finally, we'd explore the medically related context of the consumer. What tools and sites are they turning to for their information? How are they collaborating with others on health issues? How are their views and expectations on health care being shaped? We'd be sure not to be dismissive even if consumers were using tools that were demonstrably unreliable. The history of innovation shows that things can start out crummy but keep improving and vanquish those who turned up their noses.

While the list of technologies to monitor might seem daunting, it is likely that most of the necessary knowledge and expertise is already inside most hospital organizations (though it will be important to be on guard about potential blind spots—especially regarding technology that might challenge the organization's conventional wisdom or are being driven by forces outside the health care industry). The question is whether the expertise has been captured and synthesized into a coherent fact base, and whether the technology context is addressed as a fundamental factor in the strategic discussions about the business.

Some possible models for how to unearth and explore innovative technologies: The Columbus Regional Hospital in Ohio, for one, has established an innovation center with an open floor plan and access to people and cutting-edge technology, so they can continually experiment with new approaches. Boston Children's Hospital has a similar program that encourages employees to come up with new ideas and provides resources for exploring them. The hospital recently began sending robots home with urology surgical patients to do follow-up evaluations. At the moment, the robot mostly provides videoconferencing with the doctor, who can make sure medicine is being taken appropriately as well as see if a urine bag is full and needs to be changed. In the future, the hospital intends to add diagnostic equipment to check blood pressure, do urine analysis, and so on.

Having worked through the extensive detail of the technology context, hospitals should imagine all sorts of doomsday scenarios.

A big doomsday to consider is what would happen if some sort of new, nightmarish competitor enters the market through an aggressive consolidation strategy. This could be, for example, a national hospital chain or integrated network. The entrant might acquire physician practices, hospitals, imaging facilities, labs, extended care facilities, and so on and dominate the most profitable lines of care. (This nightmare is already playing out in some areas, as one health care executive told us. He likened the consolidation that is happening in some markets to the frantic community bank consolidations following the savings-and-loan crisis of the 1980s.)

Another doomsday scenario could involve someone else gaining control of all the data that patients are churning out and winding up with a huge amount of insight and, thus, control. That doomsday could be because a national company such as Kaiser Permanent wins, because a local hospital gets the business, because a new type of competitor arises, because government claims ownership, because insurers somehow intervene, etc. Whatever the case, the result could be that hospitals would be operating largely in someone else's world, offering piecemeal services and competing on cost and results much more than they do now.

Taking out a clean sheet of paper to imagine the best possible future, a hospital chain would try to truly set aside all the constraints that hospitals operate under today. Different strains of thinking might guide the designs. Perhaps a hospital would imagine a world with perfect information—a world that we can begin to imagine because of our former colleague Larry Smarr.

When Smarr walked into his doctor's office for an appointment a few years ago, the doctor asked, "What are the symptoms?" Smarr answered: "I don't have symptoms. I have data."

He did, too. Lots and lots of data. Smarr had had his DNA sequenced. He had also been monitoring all his vital signs for years, including frequent collection and analysis of stool samples. Smarr isn't just interested in his health for personal reasons. He runs a lab at the University of California, San Diego, and at UC-Irvine that is designed to simulate a computing environment 10 years in the future and that has led him to think about issues such as the possibility of having perfect information on patients.

Smarr has a history of prescience. Among other things, when he ran the Supercomputing Center at the University of Illinois, he set up a group that developed the first Web browser, known as Mosaic. When the leader of that group, Marc Andreessen, took the concept to Silicon Valley, Mosaic became Netscape and launched the Internet boom of the mid- to late 1990s. And Smarr believes that his data-not-symptoms approach will revolutionize medicine—as he puts it, the approach will finally provide what he boldly calls "a scientific basis for medicine."

He notes that we used to wait to deal with cars until we saw smoke coming from the engine but now have so many diagnostic tools that we can spot problems before they happen and can identify even subtle issues that can lead quickly to better design. Now, cars may last for 200,000 miles. Smarr believes that, in essence, wiring humans as cars have been over the past couple of decades will lead to analogous change. We'll see problems before they happen, will understand problems more deeply and will be able to give ourselves longer and healthier lives.

In the sort of world Smarr envisions, it could be possible to know about every vital sign of every patient at every moment. Doctors would be able to communicate with patients and diagnose them based not solely on their knowledge, but on total knowledge of all studies that have been conducted about symptoms, diagnoses, and alternative treatments. (This knowledge about studies may not be that far off.

IBM says that it has sent Watson to medical school, meaning that the computer program that vanquished the best Jeopardy players has been absorbing and learning to process every available bit of information on medicine—and it can read 200 million pages a second.)

A very powerful concept could, thus, be drawn on a clean sheet of paper that imagined how to serve the Larry Smarrs of the world.

Perhaps a hospital would also come up with a design based on the more limited notion of remote medicine, where doctors could not only view patients and talk with them over video links but could actually treat them; perhaps even surgery could be done remotely, with some sort of surgical robot picking up the movements of a surgeon's hands in New York and transferring those movements to a machine that operates on a patient in a remote part of North Dakota that would otherwise be unlikely to have access to a top surgeon.

Hospitals could imagine new models designed to deal with the increasing demand for care and the increasing complexity as our population ages, and as the relative health profile of the whole population continues to deteriorate.

Those are just a few possible threads. The smart doctors and business executives would have many more ideas to consider if given a clean sheet of paper and enticed out of their focus on today's issues.

Those exercises would lead right in to starting small. The hospital corporation would recognize the power of finance operations, especially in a world like hospitals, where the fixed costs are so high and charges can be allocated in a wild array of ways. To fulfill our first task, "killing" all the finance guys, the hospital would, among other things, have them quantify all sorts of doomsday scenarios to show what would happen if major, profitable streams of business moved elsewhere.

Getting everyone on the same page might prove to be even more difficult, because there are an awful lot of moving parts in a hospital. It's not possible to even talk about "doctors," because different types can have very different agendas. Highly paid anesthesiologists and specialists may have very different ideas than general surgeons do.[115] If we had to guess from a distance, though, we'd suspect that a radical new approach such as remote medicine or complete knowledge could be worked out with the hospital staff, especially with many years to plan ahead.

Our future histories speculating on who thwarted an innovation might, thus, focus on regulatory issues. States and localities will resist many changes as they try to preserve local jobs. State medical boards will try to keep, say, that New York surgeon from practicing in North Dakota, so that a surgeon in North Dakota gets the work, even if she isn't as skilled. Boards representing doctors will also likely try to keep work from moving away from their members, whether the work goes to nurses, computers or doctors in Mumbai, no matter how strong the rationale for the shift. Pharmaceutical companies might also show up in our future histories. The companies sponsor lots of research but want to hide any studies that don't show that a drug or treatment works, so they could be expected to resist a complete-knowledge scenario. There would be many more possibilities covered in the future histories, helping the hospital identify constituencies it would need to court.

In setting up a basket of killer options, the hospital chain would look at the doomsday scenarios and clean sheets of paper and come up with three or so plausible directions to test. The company might test the possibility that it could go international and become a hub, maybe *the* hub, for remote diagnosis and treatment. The company would also want to explore the possibility that it could become a hub, maybe *the* hub, for the huge new flows of information that are becoming available. Maybe the company would consider a total change in business model from fee-for-service and imagine being paid for prevention, not cure.

---

115 A doctor friend told us a joke years ago that isn't directly relevant but that illustrates how doctors differ much more than those of us outside the profession might realize. Using the term "medical doctors" to describe those who diagnose and prescribe medications, he said:" "Medical doctors know everything but can do little. Surgeons know little but can do everything. Pathologists know everything and can do everything, but it's too late." Our friend, for the record, is a surgeon.

To start to Learn Fast, the company would then break the options down into small components that could be tested. The hospital chain might conduct some sort of a test project with IBM to see just how good Watson really is and how fast it's likely to improve. The company might try remote diagnosis on its own in a variety of areas—locally, in different parts of the country, and around the globe—to test both the opportunities and the problems. To minimize expense, the company might try to piggyback on the work that MDLiveCare and Online Care are doing as they roll out limited forms of telemedicine throughout the United States.[116] The hospital chain might pick a decent-sized local corporation and take over responsibility for employees' health, just to get a sense of how costs would change and what benefits could be quantified.

The hospital might also explore setting up centers to learn what it would take to serve the Larry Smarrs, i.e., the lead users willing to be test subjects for digital medicine. Here, the hospital could learn from the efforts of start-ups like WellnessFX, which takes clients through an extensive series of diagnostics to create a series of biomarker baselines and then provides tools and consulting services that focus on health and prevention. Another start-up that might be of interest, MD Revolution, merges traditional medicine with nutrition, fitness, genomics, and extensive health-tracking technology.

The hospital would make sure to start with prototyping; there would be no hint that any individual option was the anointed model for the future of the business. Prototyping is especially tricky in the world of health care. One bright line concerns when to involve real patients, at which point medically accepted protocols must be followed. But a lot of prototyping can be done before that point, to really understand the details and potential implications of an idea.

---

116   Fasano, *Transforming Health Care.*

Demos are a critical element. Demos from a patient's viewpoint could show how it felt to be treated in a world of complete knowledge or telemedicine or one where the focus was solely on total health. Demos might also be done from other standpoints. For instance, if a certain type of doctor was expected to resist change, a demo from the doctors' perspective might be done, just to understand what they were being asked to do differently.

As more was learned, both about the technological possibilities and about the changing market, a radical innovation might be chosen and turned into a pilot. Even when we move into pilots, the goal is to learn as much as possible while spending as little as possible. If, for instance, a hospital set up a pilot that contracted with a local corporation to provide a certain standard of health for its employees, getting into preventive care and far away from fee-for-service, the hospital would change nothing about its staff or facilities. The hospital would just have existing staff act as though they were dedicated to the contract. The hospital might, at most, clear out space in a facility so the staff involved in the pilot could meet from time to time.

Learning would be celebrated, whether it was good news or bad. The hospital would have regular reviews to see what was being learned.

At this point, the devil's advocate would step up his involvement. He would have already pushed on the doomsday scenario to make sure it was comprehensive and appropriately apocalyptic and on the clean sheet of paper to make sure it was visionary, not incremental. The devil's advocate would also have asked tough questions about whether finance was demanding detailed numbers too early in the process and whether the company was truly facing up to potential deal-breakers when thinking about what groups might oppose change. The devil's advocate would have provided counsel as options were identified and testing begun, mostly to make sure that no one was jumping to premature conclusions and either plunging ahead with an idea or tabling it unfairly. But at this final stage, before rolling out an idea publicly, the devil's advocate would convene top management and run through the sort of SASE review that we described in detail in the previous chapter. That would either result in additional questions or a go-ahead.

The odds, we're willing to bet, are that a hospital would be able to carve out an important role for itself by inventing a future that patients will love—something that might resemble a network of professionals dedicated to their health, in terms of diet and exercise as well as medications; able to diagnose and treat problems remotely based on moment-by-moment data from a patient's body while relying on the latest clinical studies and best computer search capabilities; all while available 24/7.

Not every hospital company will succeed, obviously, especially if we're right that technology will carve a lot of the profitable pieces out of hospitals. In addition, some hospital chains have a big head start—Cleveland Clinic, for instance, is building clinics in Dubai and elsewhere around the world, has a terrific reputation and has stayed ahead of cost pressures by driving down expenses while providing stellar care. But we're confident that most hospital chains will follow the old approach to innovation, creating a vacuum for others to fill. Most will jump to conclusions early, perhaps because the CEO has an intuition or because the company runs into trouble and gets desperate. Decisions will be based on an incomplete review of relevant technologies and alternatives and perhaps on the need for quarterly earnings, rather than based on a disciplined, long-term approach to generating killer apps that can transform a business and an industry.

As Warren Buffett likes to say, "When the tide goes out, you learn who isn't wearing swim trunks." Not to torture his analogy too much, but following our process will help hospitals know when the tide is going out so they can have those trunks on or, better yet, can find a new, highly important and profitable place to swim.

Conclusion

We overestimate technology in the short term and under-estimate it in the long term—even when we know that we do so. In addition to all the other factors that we've discussed, this long-cited axiom explains the failure of market leaders to leverage the disruptive technologies that we've discussed in this book.

There should be no doubt about the short-term overestimation, given the exuberance and collapse of the dot-com bubble in the early 2000s. Large companies that get caught up in overestimation tend to squander investment dollars and, more destructively, management attention by going to market with rickety products that are not ready for mainstream adoption. Take the BlackBerry PlayBook. Responding to the popularity of Apple's iPad, BlackBerry rushed a tablet to market in 2011 even though it couldn't read e-mail (users had to connect a separate BlackBerry phone to make e-mail on the tablet work). The PlayBook flopped, after soaking up investment dollars and management attention from the real battle that BlackBerry faced, which was the threat that the Apple iPhone posed to BlackBerry's core phone business.

Often, companies feel so desperate that they make ill-advised acquisitions. Microsoft did this with its $6.3 billion acquisition of aQuantive, an Internet advertising firm, in 2007. Microsoft eventually took a $6.2 billion write-down on the acquisition. News Corp also over-paid to catch up when it paid $580 million in 2005 to buy MySpace, later sold for $35 million. Time Warner got so caught up in hype that it bet everything and lost when it sold itself to AOL in 2000.

Short of the sort of corporate suicide that Time Warner committed by overestimating the speed of a disruptive trend, the longer-term underestimation can be even more dangerous to large companies. Many companies see the initial hype be disproven and assume they're fine, only to be overwhelmed when the long-term impact proves profound. That complacency put Borders and Blockbuster out of business and is threatening Best Buy and many others now.

The challenge is to maintain a level head in the midst of inevitable bubble-and-burst cycles. Don't panic, but also don't be complacent. As Peter Drucker observed:

"Contrary to popular belief, 'flashes of genius' are uncommonly rare. Purposeful innovation begins with the analysis of opportunities. The search has to be organized, and must be done on a regular, systematic basis."

Based on our research and experience, our prescription for that systematic innovation process is to Think Big, Start Small, and Learn Fast. If you can follow that prescription, you'll still overestimate in the short run and underestimate in the long run—after all, we're all human—but you'll do a far better job of sensing what's really going on in your market and of putting yourself at the forefront of the powerful trends that are transforming our economy. Others will fall by the wayside, but you will thrive.

Afterword

Moving From Innovation to Invention

The failure of Xerox to commercialize the personal computer and other technologies invented at its Palo Alto Research Center, or PARC, in the 1970s was so epic that whole books have been written about the hundreds of billions of dollars of revenue and market cap that Xerox ceded to Apple, IBM, Intel, Microsoft, and many, many others.

Except that Xerox PARC wasn't a failure. It was a roaring success. You should emulate PARC, if you can.

What people miss is that Xerox spent just $43 million (in today's dollars) on all the work that led up to the personal computer and related technologies yet came away with a business that has generated more than $100 billion of revenue for Xerox. That business was the laser printer, which was the core of Xerox's business for many years.

Yes, companies not named Xerox commercialized the personal computer, the graphical user interface, Ethernet, and other technologies invented at PARC, and you can argue that Xerox should have either brought those to market itself (unlikely, given how different they were from Xerox's core business) or at least should have figured out a way to license them and mint money.

But go back to the two key numbers: Xerox invested $43 million in research and produced a $100 billion business. That's more than $2,000 of revenue for every dollar of research. Who wouldn't love that kind of return?

The process we've laid out in this book might win you that sort of success. GE, for one, thinks it can generate enormous revenue based on one of our six megatrends, the growing ubiquity of sensors. GE is building on a concept referred to as the Internet of Things. This is the idea that all our devices will be able to talk to each other and coordinate on our behalf, without having to get us humans involved. GE sees $15 trillion of revenue up for grabs because of the developing Internet of Things.

Far more typically, though, the path to a 2,000X return is less straightforward. You'll need to move into a realm with higher risk and higher reward. You'll need to go beyond innovation and into the realm of invention.

The shift means investing in some green field based on an idea that is potentially revolutionary but that is looking far enough into the future that it is still vaguely formed. In some ways, inventing is like the approach taken by a character that Douglas Adams introduced early in *The Hitchhiker's Guide to the Galaxy.* When the character got lost while driving (in the dark ages before GPS), he simply picked out another car heading more or less in his direction and followed it. The character never quite knew where he was going but always wound up somewhere interesting.

In the case of Xerox PARC, executives had the sense in the early 1970s that tectonic plates were shifting because of developments in computing. It wasn't at all clear whether those shifts would produce just a temblor or would equate to smashing South America and Africa back together to form a new Pangaea, but Xerox decided the potential was great enough that it would assemble a small group of the greatest experts in the world and explore.

Such a group had already started to coalesce because of efforts sponsored by the federal government that were spawning the Internet. So, Xerox hired Bob Taylor, the key manager of those federal efforts, in 1970. He then assembled a dream team from the federal research and elsewhere.

These were incredibly early days in the history of personal computing. While computers were in widespread use at big companies by 1970, the inputs were punch cards, and the outputs were long print-outs. Computers were used in the back office and were attended by a sort of priestly class wearing white lab coats and working in special, air-conditioned rooms.

Taylor came on board at Xerox less than two years after Douglas Engelbart had given what is now referred to reverently in the computer world as the Mother of All Demos, where he introduced the mouse (a wooden shell covering two wheels) and bit-map graphing (the ability to have a computer assemble images on a screen out of individual dots). What we think of today as a microprocessor wasn't invented until 1971, by an Intel employee.

At Xerox, though, the notion formed that computing could be taken away from the men in lab coats and brought to everyone. This thinking came about partly because the renowned management theo-rist Peter Drucker had begun writing about what he called the knowl-edge worker. Alan Kay, who ran the team at PARC that developed the personal computer and produced many other breakthroughs, was a Drucker fan and tried to imagine the tools that his knowledge workers would need.[117] Kay came up with an image he called the Dynabook. Although computers in those days were enormous and although the Internet consisted of just a few computers hooked together on

---

117 We had the privilege of being at a lunch of some 10 people where Kay told Drucker that his knowledge-worker concept had shaped the early PC work. Drucker was surprised and delighted. Kay did tell us later that, while the knowledge worker was a useful construct for him, he never really believed that business people would be the early adopters of PCs. He felt they had too much to unlearn. He believed that children should be the real focus and developed the PC with them in mind.

college campuses, Kay imagined a device that would be light, mobile, battery-powered, with a good color screen and a keyboard, and that would have access both to other computers and to a nearly unlimited amount of information. Essentially, more than four decades ago, he imagined a laptop of today with a Wi-Fi connection to the Internet. He set about building the Dynabook, and all kinds of important inventions fell out of the work—the personal computer itself, the graphical user interface, overlapping windows, object-oriented programming, the laser printer (developed by a team other than Kay's) and Ethernet (developed principally by Bob Metcalfe).

Now, it might be easy to say that imagining today's Wi-Fi–enabled laptop forty years ago is such a staggering act of genius that it's not even worth trying to replicate. Kay is, in fact, extraordinary, as were many of his colleagues at PARC. Perhaps fifteen years ago, we came up with an idea about putting a tiny device on car keys that could be made to chirp anytime you were looking for them, and a friend said, "Oh, Alan had that idea twenty years ago." He quickly added: "But if you're only twenty years behind Alan Kay, you're doing really well."

Kay himself argues that the successes at Xerox PARC can be duplicated in many companies. He says that finding people like him actually isn't the hard part. In just about every field, it's possible to identify the smartest people. They generally thrive by working with each other, so it's easy to get them to join a team. The trick is to establish the right dynamics for the team and the right relationship with the corporate parent.

While the idea of inventing, and not just innovating, may some day merit a book of its own, here we'll just lay out the basic principles, based mostly on conversations with Kay and on some consulting work we've done that at least borders on invention.

The work obviously begins with defining some sort of field. That's reasonably hard to do, given that, if the locations for breakthroughs were known, you wouldn't need to invent them, and everybody would be going after them just as hard as you are. Almost any field is possible as long as the potential for breakthroughs is sufficiently large and as long as there is at least some relationship with your business—a la Xerox copiers and the state of electronics in 1970.

Medicine is surely an area where many companies should invest in invention. Many invest heavily in R&D, obviously, but they tend to try to build on the drugs and devices that they already make; there is room out there for someone to construct a Xerox PARC for medicine, come up with a 30-year-out concept like the Dynabook, try to build it, and watch the inventions come tumbling out of the work. Companies that make home appliances might assemble a group around the concept of the home of the future. Similar concepts could drive other invention: the future of work, the office of the future, shopping in 2040, and so on. Just about any company could try to invent responses to what is being described as a coming age of resource scarcity. China, alone, is building 2 ½ cities the size of Chicago every year for the foreseeable future, and some 2.5 billion people around the world will join the middle class by 2030, which will place unbelievable demands on the world's resources—while creating huge opportunities for anyone smart enough to relieve the problems.[118]

Once a general direction is identified, it helps to establish a grand goal, a la Xerox and the Dynabook. Work in science sometimes takes this approach. A prize may be awarded for the first plane to fly around the world without refueling. The goal is so extreme that invention has to happen—even if none of us will ever fly 24,000 miles as Dick Rutan and Jeana Yeager did in 1986, spending more than nine days in a cramped structure that weighed only one-ninth as much as the gasoline it held at

---

118 There is a little advertising going on here. Paul is helping with a book being written by Stefan Heck and Matt Rogers on the resource problem and its solutions. The title is *Resource Revolution*. It is currently set for release in the spring of 2014. Watch for it.

takeoff and that had only a few gallons left in its tanks when it touched down. NASA and its grand goals have spun out numerous inventions, including Velcro and the compound that became Armor All. Steven Chu, a Nobel Prize-winning physicist who became the secretary of Energy, reorganized the department's system of national labs by giving each a grand goal. For instance, one now focuses on coming up with a new form of photosynthesis that will let algae secrete fuel in high volumes that could be used to power cars.

As we've said, it's key to set the right relationship between the company and the research team and to have the right manager of those links. Xerox, after doing brilliant work at PARC in the early PC days, reacted too strongly to criticisms of the money it left on the table with the inventions it didn't bring to market. Xerox tried to fit PARC too directly into its product development and smothered the approach to invention. It's only in the past decade or so that Xerox has again given PARC free rein, and that PARC is again doing pioneering work, in artificial intelligence and other areas. IBM's research arm went through a similar arc. It did profound work in the 1970s and 1980s, winning two Nobel Prizes, then became too closely tied to product goals, then was given more room to roam and began producing breakthroughs such as the Deep Blue chess-playing computer that defeated Garry Kasparov, the Watson computer that beat the best Jeopardy players in the world, and the pieces that are feeding IBM's Smarter Planet push.[119]

Bob Taylor at Xerox PARC is the best model we've seen for thinking about how to give a team the right amount of leeway while making sure they play nicely with each other and stay focused enough to complete projects. You might also look to the leaders of the Manhattan Project, about whom much more has been written. Gen. Leslie Groves, while not the least bit technical, did a beautiful job of both managing the scien-

---

119 PARC now pays part of its own freight by consulting on innovation. Some of
      the IBM research can be viewed as product development and even marketing
      for the company's consulting arm, which works on Smarter Planet projects.

tists and of managing the bosses in Washington. Robert Oppenheimer, a spectacular physicist, had the respect of those who worked for him and had the discernment to keep the work on the atomic bomb from heading down too many rabbit trails.

When you set goals, make sure you're realistic. Realize that you'll lose all the money you invest in most of your projects (a problem you minimize by keeping projects small). Even the successful projects won't pay dividends for years. If you're just focused on your company's or unit's performance over the next year or two, don't invest in invention. Xerox didn't bring a laser printer to market until 1977, seven years after the work at PARC began. C. Peter McColough, the CEO of Xerox at the time that PARC began its work, deserves the credit for the investment that led to a huge business at Xerox—but the credit was a long time coming.

As for the team itself, aim high. You may not be like the Manhattan Project and assemble Richard Feynman, Edward Teller, and John von Neumann, with Albert Einstein lurking in the background, but you should have the project manager aim for the very best in the world. She'll know who they are and be able to pull many of them in if the project is important enough.

When you've assembled the team, you need to have them in one location, even in our increasingly virtual world. People react differently and more broadly when they see each other in the hall or the cafeteria than they do if someone holds a call or a virtual meeting with a defined agenda. Considerable research into Bell Labs in the days when it was inventing the transistor and so much else found that much of the magic came from chance encounters by experts that produced sparks. Former DOE Secretary Chu has designed the national labs so that experts from various fields will have to bump into each other. Steve Jobs designed the main building at Pixar so that everyone would be funneled in and out the same way and would strike up conversations.

Some companies take a short cut on invention by relying on government to do the basic research or allying with universities, whose work generally draws on government funds. In many cases, government and universities can be great sources for invention. The Defense Advanced Research Projects Agency (DARPA), the research arm of the US Department of Defense, gave us the Internet, GPS, and many other innovations. The Advanced Research Projects Agency–Energy (ARPA-E), the young research arm of the US Department of Energy that's modeled on DARPA, has even set up mechanisms to help turn its research into commercial opportunities.

Still, if research comes from some public source, then everyone has access to it. Any company can build on the Internet or GPS.

By contrast, if you're the company that invents the future of medicine, you will have the inside track on that 2,000X return.

Glossary

Big Data
See Emergent Knowledge.

Circuit-Switching Network
A network in which bandwidth is reserved for a single communication (such as a telephone call), and only as long as that communication lasts. Compare with Packet-Switching Network.

The Cloud
A colloquial term for a centralized network of computers, servers and data storage systems, which users can take advantage of in lieu of relying entirely on local resources (such as the hardware and software on the user's computer).

Cloud Computing
Computing tasks (such as the accessing of files or applications) that are performed by accessing The Cloud.

Devil's Advocate
An individual or group within an organization whose role is to assess all critical assumptions, key forecasts and other make-or-break aspects of a potential killer app.

Emergent Knowledge
New categories of knowledge previously impractical, or impossible, to use on a regular basis but now enabled by the analysis of data collected through embedded sensors, connected devices and other advances in information technology.

Groupthink
A term for mistakes and fallacies that result from decision making processes that are conducted by groups rather than individuals.

Incumbent
A large, established company (as opposed to smaller and ostensibly more agile startup companies).

Intrapreneur
Individuals who behave and innovate like entrepreneurs while working within a large organization.

Killer App
Products so revolutionary that they cause massive creative destruction and huge shifts in revenue and market value.

Knowledge Navigator
An early conception of the iPad, which was developed at Apple long before the processing power necessary for the iPad became available.

Law of Disruption
An informal law that states that, because humans develop incrementally while technology grows exponentially, rapid advances in technology will periodically cause upheaval.

Massively Open Online Course

Publicly available college courses that use the internet to offer course materials such as lectures, syllabi and readings.

MOOC

An abbreviation for Massively Open Online Course.

Moore's Law

An informal law that states that, over the history of computing hardware, the number of transistors on a chip will double approximately every two years.

Option

a contract conveying a right to buy or sell designated securities, commodities, or property interest at a specified price during a stipulated period.

Packet-Switching Network

A network (such as the internet) in which bandwidth is constantly active, and in which communications are broken down into 'packets' which contain information about the recipient and about the order in which the information is to be reassembled. Compare with Circuit-Switching Network.

PBM

An abbreviation of Pharmacy Benefits Managers.

Pharmacy Benefits Managers

Intermediaries that negotiate better prices for corporate insurance plans, and that have put pressure on retailers such as Walgreen's by steering consumers toward the Internet for repeat medicine purchases.

Pilot
A test version of a product or service for which there is an expectation of the test becoming the final product or service. Compare with Prototype.

Prototype
A test version of a product or service for which there is no expectation of the test becoming the final product or service. Compare with Pilot.

Reed's Law
A law that explains why group-forming networks (such as social networking sites) tend to grow much more rapidly than person-to-person networks (like telephones or e-mails) or broadcast networks (like television).

SAS
A process for moderating workshops that encourages free expression and the challenging of assumptions. Short for "Strategic Assumptions Surfacing and Testing".

Showrooming
The practice of browsing for items in a physical store and then purchasing products online for better prices.

Telemedicine
The use of medical information exchanged from one site to another via electronic communications (such as video, e-mail, smartphones, etc.) to improve a patient's clinical health status.

The Internet of Things

The idea that devices will someday be equipped with the technology to communicate and coordinate with each other without human involvement.

VC

An abbreviation for Venture Capitalist.

22603185R00126

Made in the USA
Charleston, SC
24 September 2013